Distilled Knowledge

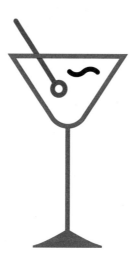

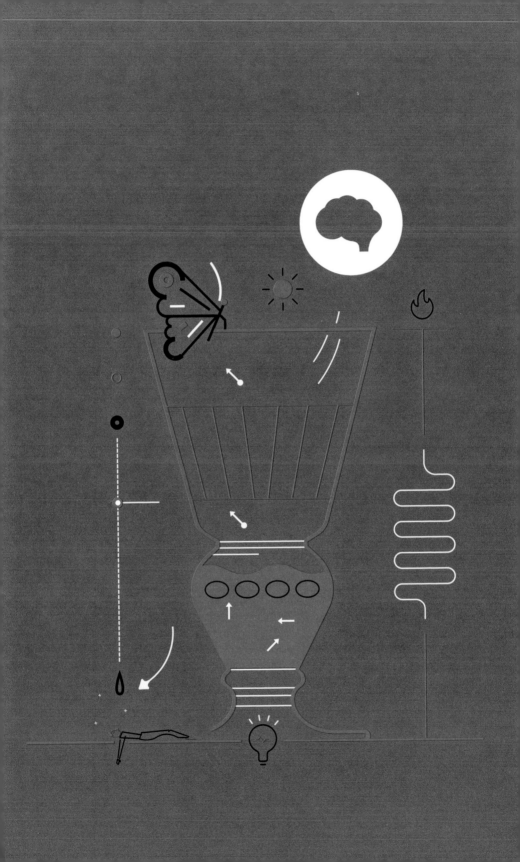

Brian D. Hoefling

Illustrations by Leandro Castelao

Distilled
Knowledge

The Science Behind

Drinking's

Greatest Myths,

Legends,

and Unanswered Questions

Abbeville Press Publishers
New York   London

*For my parents, whose pride and support
I have never doubted, and who,
having no idea what they were getting into,
first taught me to drink.*

Editor: Shannon Lee Connors
Copy editor: Amy Hughes
Designer: Misha Beletsky
Composition: Angela Taormina
Production manager: Louise Kurtz

First published in 2016 by
Abbeville Press, 116 West 23rd Street, New York, NY 10011.

First edition
10 9 8 7 6 5 4 3 2 1

ISBN 978-0-7892-1268-9

Library of Congress Cataloging-in-Publication Data is available
upon request.

For bulk and premium sales and for text adoption procedures, write
to Customer Service Manager, Abbeville Press, 116 West 23rd Street,
New York, NY 10011, or call 1-800-ARTBOOK.

Visit Abbeville Press online at www.abbeville.com.

Contents

Apéritifs

Preface

Introduction

Preface

There's no shortage of scientific (or pseudoscientific) discussion about alcohol in our world. Pick up any bar guide or talk to any barfly, and eventually a theory of solution chemistry or human ethanol metabolism will be trotted out for your benefit. Sometimes these claims are even true—though it can be hard to tell which ones. Consider:

"You should never add water to whiskey." (*False.*)

"Carbonated mixers get you drunker." (*True.*)

"A hangover is a dehydrated brain." (*Partially.*) (*Sometimes.*) (*A hangover is a lot of things.*)

The maddening thing is, all the information you could want about drinking is out there. Scientists and industry professionals have done the research, but it's hard to know where to look to get the answers—particularly if you have a lot of questions.

I know this from experience. Drinking has a remarkable ability to stimulate my academic interest (along with conversation and the desire to drink more). I've been geeking out about cocktail recipes and booze history since college; it was only a matter of time before I started looking into the science.

Off and on, at odd hours over the course of several years, I tried to dig up information on alcohol "facts" I'd never heard substantiated. Most of the time I was researching things that supposedly affect how drunk you get—carbonation, heat, the gold flakes in Goldschläger, and so on. It surprised me that there was no one-stop shop where I could get my questions answered.

That was the kernel that germinated into this book. It took a couple of years and a fortuitous conversation with a dear friend before "Somebody should write a book about that" finally turned into "*I* should write a book about that"—and so *Distilled Knowledge* was born. If it saves even one person a few hours of frustrated Googling, I'll be happy.

What Is This Book?

Distilled Knowledge is a compendium of basic scientific information that pertains to alcohol at all stages—from first fermentation to the last dregs of your hangover. I hope to answer common questions, put disputes to rest, and perhaps prompt some of you to further research on your own.

What Isn't This Book?

Oh, so many things. It isn't a work of original scientific scholarship. I am not a scientist; I come at this topic from the other side—I'm a barfly, like you. What you're holding is my best understanding of the science that's already out there. If you're obsessive enough, you can find all this information yourself, by digging through library stacks and scouring the Internet—believe me, I know. I wrote this book so you won't have to do all that.

It isn't a cocktail book or a guide to bar techniques. There are no recipes in these pages (not even as Easter eggs for those of you who assume I'm being facetious—you know who you are). If you're looking for recipes presented with a scientific flair, I recommend Dave Arnold's *Liquid Intelligence* or Kevin Liu's *Craft Cocktails at Home*.

It also isn't the only book in the world that looks at alcohol from a scientific perspective. If you'd like to read more on the topic but don't want to dive directly into the technical literature, Adam Rogers's *Proof* is an excellent next move. If you're one of those people who enjoys eating as well as drinking, Harold McGee's magisterial *On Food and Cooking* is an invaluable reference to the whats and hows of both.

How Do I Use This Book?

Distilled Knowledge is structured so that it can be read straight through or consulted as a reference text. Each chapter is divided into sections that address particular topics. Where necessary, they're cross-referenced with other sections or the Appendix for further reading—just follow the martini glasses.⍦

⍦
Bottoms up!

I've tried to include at least a quick-and-dirty version of whatever background explanation you may need in each section. That way, if you're jumping around, you won't have to go back and read prior sections to understand what you're looking at; and if you're going straight through, you'll know which of the things you've already learned will be specifically relevant to what you're reading. You'll also find a handy list of references in the back of this book, as well as footnotes that point you toward specific studies I mention.

Who Should Read This Book?

Everyone, naturally! My goal is for people at all levels of expertise to find something to appreciate. But *Distilled Knowledge* will probably be most helpful to the curious amateur, the person who knows just enough about science or alcohol to know that there's much more to learn.

Introduction

Everything You Need to Know about Alcohol, in about Twelve Hundred Words

If you're reading this book, you've probably had an adult beverage or two in your lifetime. Maybe you've even taken the time to read the labels on your bottles or to chat with your bartender. In other words, there's a pretty good chance you know the basics of what alcohol is, how it's made, and so on. If you feel confident in your background knowledge, feel free to skip ahead to chapter 1.

Y

Chapter 1,
Fermenta-
tion, p. 19

If, however, you want to brush up on the fundamentals before moving on, this introduction should get you up to speed.

What Is Alcohol?

Chemically, an alcohol is an organic molecule that has a hydroxyl group (an oxygen atom connected to a hydrogen atom) attached to a saturated carbon atom:

Methanol: The simplest alcohol.

(You can forget that definition right away if you like—we're not going to bother with it again.) In organic chemistry, you can tell which kind of chemical something is by its suffix; alcohols have names that end in -ol.

When we talk about alcohol in our daily lives, we're pretty much always referring to ethanol, a structurally simple alcohol that makes us feel nice when we drink it:

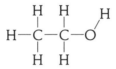

Ethanol: The second-simplest alcohol.

Ethanol mixes with water in any proportion—and since you're mostly water, it spreads throughout your entire body pretty quickly. Ethanol does some funny things to your body and your mind along the way, and it's particularly mischievous in its dealings with your central nervous system. You know this as "getting drunk."

Ethanol is naturally produced by a variety of microorganisms, most of which are yeasts. These microorganisms consume sugars and they produce, among other things, both ethanol and carbon dioxide. This process is one example of the broader suite of microbial activities that we call *fermentation*. Leavened bread, vinegar, and many other nonalcoholic products are made by different kinds of fermentation, but let's leave those aside for now.

Alcoholic beverages made by fermentation include wine (made from grapes), beer (made from cereal grains, especially barley), cider (made from apples), sake (made from rice), and mead (made from honey). Anything that contains sugar can be fermented under the right circumstances—carrots, milk, palm tree sap, you name it.

Humans have been taking advantage of fermentation for thousands of years. More recently, people figured out that they could separate the liquids in a fermented mixture by boiling and recondensing them, resulting in a finished product with a higher concentration of alcohol. This process is called *distillation*. The tool we use for distilling is a *still*.

Alcoholic beverages made by distillation are often referred to as *hard liquors*, a category that includes brandy (made from grapes), whiskey (made from cereal grains), rum (made from sugarcane and its derivatives), and tequila (made from blue agave—which is not, as some people seem to think, a cactus). Vodka and gin (generally, but not necessarily, made from grains) also fall under this heading.

Ethanol usually makes up between 5 and 15 percent of the volume of a fermented drink. This measurement is commonly expressed as *alcohol by volume*, or ABV. It means exactly the same thing either way—about 14 percent of the liquid in a 14 percent ABV bottle of wine is ethanol.

Another measurement of ethanol content in alcoholic beverages is *proof*. It's usually used to describe distilled spirits, and is represented by the degree symbol (°). The simplest way to remember what proof means is to think of it as twice the ABV of a given spirit. A vodka that is 40 percent alcohol by volume would be 80 proof, which might be written on the bottle as 80°. That's a standard proof for distilled spirits, though hard liquors are often bottled as low as 70° or as high as 120°, and there's a whole class of rums bottled at 151° specifically.

Hard liquor comes in bottles of various sizes; two of the most common are the *fifth* and the *handle*.

A fifth is a 750-milliliter (mL) bottle. Spirits used to be sold in bottles that held one-fifth of a gallon; these were sensibly, if unimaginatively, called fifths. A 750 mL bottle holds just slightly less than one-fifth of a gallon, so the name stuck even as the measurements changed. A standard wine bottle holds the same volume, but it's usually referred to as a bottle rather than a fifth.

A handle is a 1.75-liter (L) bottle. Bottles this size are often, but not always, designed with a handle to make them easier to carry—which is how we get the name.

There are other categories of alcoholic beverages we haven't yet mentioned. Port, sherry, and vermouth are *fortified wines*, or wines to which a distilled spirit has been added.

Liqueurs are distilled spirits to which sugar and flavorings (usually fruit or spices) have been added. This is a very broad category. It contains purpose-made liqueurs, as varied as Chartreuse, triple sec, and Irish cream, as well as flavored versions of familiar spirits, like Plymouth's sloe gin or Patrón's tequila-based Citrónge. In the United States, if something is labeled as a cordial, schnapps, flavored brandy, cream liqueur, or crème liqueur (crème de menthe, crème de cacao, etc.), chances are it belongs in this group.

Bitters are a class of drink that is made by adding highly aromatic herbs and spices to distilled spirits (or, very occasionally, to glycerin). They tend to be quite bitter. *Potable bitters*, such as Campari, are consumed either mixed or on their own, while *nonpotable* bitters, like Angostura and Peychaud's, are used a few drops at a time to add flavor to other drinks. *Bitters* is both singular and plural.

Then of course there are *cocktails*, which are combinations of the various liquids I've mentioned thus far with fruits, herbs, syrups, nonalcoholic beverages, and each other. Cocktails usually have a hard liquor as their primary ingredient (often called the *base spirit*), as is the case with the whiskey in an Old Fashioned or the gin in a Martini. A cocktail is a single-serving drink; a similar beverage made in much larger quantities would be a *punch*.

Finally, a note on terminology: *spirits* and *liquor* have slightly fluid meanings. Most of the time, they specifically imply hard liquor; but they can also be used to refer to the whole universe of alcoholic beverages. To spare us all the trouble of endlessly repeating the phrase, "beer, wine, and spirits," which is also not comprehensive, I'll use these terms in their more inclusive sense from time to time throughout the book. The meaning should always be clear from the context.

If you would like a more detailed taxonomy of spirits, and don't mind getting it from an erudite curmudgeon whose brand recommendations are half a century old, I suggest you pick up a copy of David Embury's *The Fine Art of Mixing Drinks*—a classic in the field of cocktail literature. David Wondrich's *Imbibe!* also includes an excellent rundown, and I highly recommend it if you're looking for something a bit more contemporary.

Congratulations! You should now be ready to take on what the rest of this book throws at you. But if you do find yourself feeling lost or confused at any point, you can always turn to the glossary or the appendix[T] for further clarification.

Now, pour yourself a nice cold drink (or top off the one you already have), and enjoy *Distilled Knowledge*!

Y
Glossary,
p. 177,
Appendix,
p. 169

1. Fermentation

What Is Fermentation?

Strange as it may seem, given how common fermentation is and its importance in human history, we have no precise, universally agreed upon definition of what fermentation is. Scientific, commercial, and common-parlance definitions don't overlap perfectly; our working definition here will be a bit of a compromise among the three.

Fermentation, of course, isn't limited to the production of alcohol—if it were we'd have to exclude vinegar from the category of fermented goods. But regardless of the final product, fermentation definitely does require the action of a microorganism, such as a yeast or bacterium. It often takes place in the absence of oxygen, although the most common strains of yeast used in ethanol production will happily keep fermenting in an oxygen-rich environment.

What do all types of fermentation have in common? They're all the result of microorganisms breaking down chemicals, from large molecules to simpler ones, in order to provide energy for themselves.

In other words, fermentation is essentially a digestive process. The main ingredient in these reactions is always some kind of organic molecule—often a sugar or a starch, sometimes an alcohol—that is reduced to smaller components to release energy. The end results of fermentation are generally acids, alcohols, or gases.

The yeasts and bacteria responsible for providing us with alcohol have no knowledge of the brewing process and limited interest in it. From their perspective, the chemicals we consider desirable, such as ethanol and acetic acid, are either waste by-products or defensive secretions meant to make the local environment hostile to every organism but them. In other words, for yeasts and bacteria it's a fight for survival—which, though microscopic, is playing out constantly in all corners of the world, yielding all the fascinating flavors of fermentation and, of course, the alcohol itself.

Yeast Fermentation

Ethanol can be produced synthetically from petroleum products, but the overwhelming majority of ethanol in the world (including every drop you drink) is still made by microorganisms and mostly by yeast.

Yeasts are single-celled fungi. There are hundreds of species of yeasts, and they're absolutely everywhere. Some juices will ferment naturally if you just leave them out; palm sap, for instance, becomes palm wine within hours of harvesting due to the actions of airborne yeasts.

Yeasts used in the commercial production of alcohol are most often carefully cultivated strains with known characteristics. They are almost invariably members of the genus *Saccharomyces* and often varieties of the species *cerevisiae*.

Countertop Fermentation

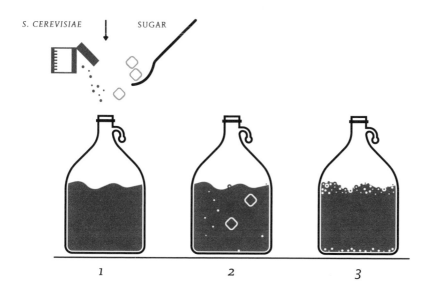

S. CEREVISIAE   SUGAR

1   2   3

At its simplest, fermentation is yeast eating sugar and producing carbon dioxide and ethanol as by-products. You can easily undertake fermentation at home. Leave a glass of juice out for a few days, and you may even do it by accident!

In a low- or no-oxygen environment these yeasts will ferment glucose ($C_6H_{12}O_6$) into carbon dioxide (CO_2) and ethanol (CH_3CH_2OH), releasing energy that the yeasts can then use. The chemical formula for this process is:

$$C_6H_{12}O_6 \rightarrow 2\ CH_3CH_2OH + 2\ CO_2$$

These yeasts are also capable of a related process called respiration, which turns glucose into water and carbon dioxide. This also provides the yeast with energy, but requires oxygen to work, as we can see in this formula:

$$C_6H_{12}O_6 + 6\ O_2 \rightarrow 6\ H_2O + 6\ CO_2$$

Respiration is more efficient at generating energy than fermentation is, but several *Saccharomyces* species prefer fermentation even when oxygen is available, because the resulting ethanol slows the growth of other competing organisms. *S. cerevisiae* is particularly well suited to living with a slight buzz and will tend to outlast other species of ethanol-tolerant yeast.

Yeasts get energy from fermentation, but like all living things they have other biological processes and need various nutrients to survive. This is a very good thing for the brewer, vintner, or spirits producer, because those other processes are what produce fermentation's flavors.

Think of rum, made from a source as close to pure glucose as any in the world. How do some rums end up with banana flavors? It's not quite as simple as "The yeast made them!" But what you're tasting (isoamyl acetate, chemically speaking) is in there only because of the biological needs and processes of the particular microbes working on the juice.

Stopping Yeast Fermentation

Fermentation will end naturally if the yeast runs out of sugar or other essential nutrients, or produces enough ethanol to make the mixture toxic to itself (around 14 to 18 percent by volume, depending on the strain). It's sometimes desirable to cut the process short sooner, usually to retain some unfermented sugars or to control which yeast-produced flavors are in the final product.

One of the easiest ways to put the brakes on fermentation is to adjust the temperature of the mixture. Depending on the desired product and the strain of yeast, the ideal fermenting temperature may be anywhere from fifty to eighty degrees Fahrenheit.

While yeasts will continue to work under hotter conditions than they prefer, the particular flavors they produce may change, and these variations are usually undesirable. *S. cerevisiae* can still grow in conditions above one hundred degrees Fahrenheit—the species is very heat-tolerant as well as very ethanol-tolerant—but temperatures well below boiling are still hot enough to kill it.

Chilling, on the other hand, can slow or stop fermentation without reaching a temperature that kills the microorganisms. *S. cerevisiae* can even survive being frozen.

The difficulty from the brewer's perspective is that chilled yeasts are only dormant, and an increase in temperature can reactivate them. If you want to stop the fermentation permanently, you'll need to incorporate some kind of filtration process or keep your beer just above freezing forever.[T]

Most fun of all is arresting by fortification, or adding distilled liquor before the fermentation finishes. This stops the process while some of the sugars have yet to be fermented, and is the reason that port wine, which is fortified with a neutral spirit made from grapes, is both stronger and sweeter than an ordinary wine.

Filtration and Fining, p. 31

Other Fermenting Agents

Ethanol is primarily a yeast derivative, and *S. cerevisiae* is a particularly prominent yeast species, but we've by no means exhausted the list of organisms involved in fermentation.

To begin with, *Saccharomyces* refers to an entire genus of yeasts that, in addition to *S. cerevisiae*, contains several other species that are important in fermentation. *S. florentinus* is involved in

Fermentation Flavor Wheel

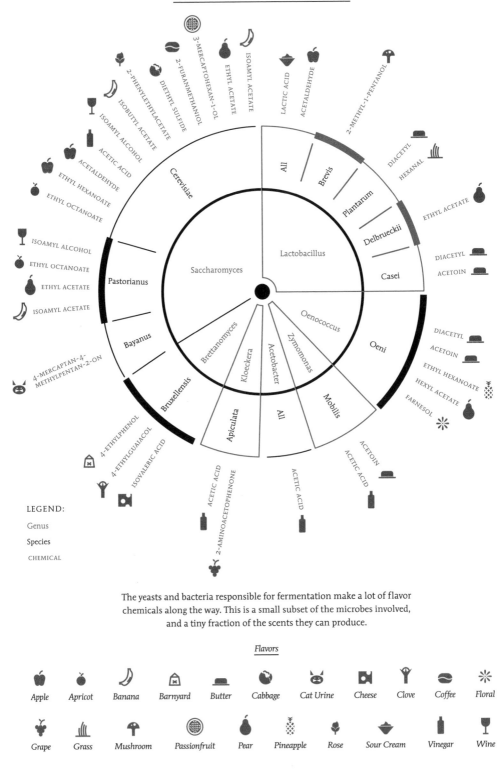

The yeasts and bacteria responsible for fermentation make a lot of flavor chemicals along the way. This is a small subset of the microbes involved, and a tiny fraction of the scents they can produce.

Flavors

Apple · Apricot · Banana · Barnyard · Butter · Cabbage · Cat Urine · Cheese · Clove · Coffee · Floral

Grape · Grass · Mushroom · Passionfruit · Pear · Pineapple · Rose · Sour Cream · Vinegar · Wine naturally fermenting ginger beer. *S. pastorianus* is commonly used in brewing lager beer. *S. bayanus*, with its naturally high alcohol tolerance, is a favorite in the production of stronger wines and ciders.

Expanding our view, we encounter genera of wild yeasts like *Kloeckera* and *Brettanomyces*. Both are involved in the production of Belgian lambic beers, and *Kloeckera* can be desirable in wild-fermented wine. *Brettanomyces bruxellensis*, which produces aromas reminiscent of a barnyard, is either important to the character of certain European red wines or a scourge that must be wiped off the face of the earth, depending on which vintner you ask.

Then there are the bacteria. *Zymomonas mobilis*, for instance, shares with yeasts the ability to turn glucose into ethanol and carbon dioxide. Along with *S. cerevisiae*, it is involved in the production of *pulque*, the fermented agave sap that is to tequila what wine is to brandy. In the making of palm wine, *Zymomonas mobilis* is actually a more effective agent of fermentation than yeasts.

Some bacteria, including members of the genera *Lactobacillus* and *Oenococcus*, are known for producing lactic acid by fermentation. They're involved in the production of everything from yogurt to sake to sauerkraut. The species *Oenococcus oeni* is important in wine production, in which it is responsible for turning malic acid into the less-sour lactic acid. It also contributes diacetyl, the organic compound that gives Chardonnay its distinctive buttery flavor.

But the king of bacterial fermenters would have to be *Acetobacter*, known and named for producing acetic acid, the distinctive ingredient in vinegar. Species of *Acetobacter* are present in most alcoholic fermentations, for the very good reason that *Acetobacter* can survive in and metabolize ethanol. Ethanol is, in fact, what these bacteria process to make acetic acid, which is why you can make cider and wine into vinegar over time. The word *vinegar* even derives from the Old French for "sour wine."

Malting and Starch Breakdown

Yeast fermentation requires simple sugars, which are the raw materials that the yeast will turn into ethanol. If you're making wines that isn't a problem, because grapes contain sugars to begin with. Fruits are generally an easy starting point for fermentation because of their sugar content, as are honey and molasses.

But some of the world's favorite drinks are made from cereal grains, which are densely packed with long starch molecules and low on simple sugars. Corn, wheat, and rye all fall into this category, as does barley, which is the main ingredient in Scotch and Irish whiskey and a major component of many other whiskeys and many beers. So how do these starches go from grain to bottle?

Here's where we get a little lucky. First, keep in mind that sugars and starches are the same kind of molecule, carbohydrates. Sugars are simply shorter chains than starches are; turning one into the other just requires the right digestive enzyme.

Second, note that a cereal grain is a seed. Under the right conditions, it wants to try to grow a new plant. And that plant can't use complex carbohydrates for energy any better than the yeast can.

To unlock the sugars, grains that will be used to make beer and whiskey are malted before being fermented. What this means is that the seeds are put in water and allowed to sprout. As the plant emerges from the seed, it produces enzymes that break down those starches into the sugars (a process called "saccharification") it needs to grow. Barley's high enzyme activity is the reason it's so often used to make alcoholic beverages.

Once the desired balance of sugar and starch is reached, the malted grains are kilned—that is, heated and dried. This process kills the sprouts, halts the saccharification of the starches, and adds a few flavors of its own by browning the sugars. The enzymes are still in there, though; if the malt is mixed with water and other grains, they'll float around, converting starches into sugars. The resulting mixture is the "mash," and the step of creating it ("mashing") comes between malting and fermentation.

If you're drinking a commercially made beer or whiskey, you can be confident that the starches used to produce your beverage were broken down by malting before reaching your glass. But this isn't the only way to saccharify a grain.

In sake production, for instance, another microorganism, the *koji* mold, breaks down the starch in rice both before and during the yeast fermentation. And in the traditional way of preparing *chicha*, a South American drink made from fermented corn, the brewers chew the grains and contribute their salivary enzymes to the saccharification process. Unlike malting and *koji*, this method has proven difficult to industrialize.

Hops

Most fermented beverages are made from one thing—wine from grapes, hard cider from apples, sake from rice, and so on. Why, then, can't we leave well enough alone with barley in beer? Why add hops?

It's important to recognize that hops haven't always been part of beer. Their addition seems to have begun about twelve hundred years ago, and they didn't become a staple until the seventeenth century. We've been drinking beer for thousands of years longer than that.

However, throughout that whole history of beer drinking, people have been flavoring their fermented barley malt with something, be it honey, fruit, or spices. Medieval European beer was flavored with *gruit*, a mixture of cold-weather herbs that one might also find in gin. *Sahti*, beer's distinctive Finnish cousin, is still flavored with juniper berries today.

These various traditional ingredients have often been added because of medicinal properties they were believed to possess, but regardless of their efficacy they have always served to improve the drink's taste. Fermented malt is like dried pasta: heavenly with the right complements but not great on its own.

How Beer Is Made

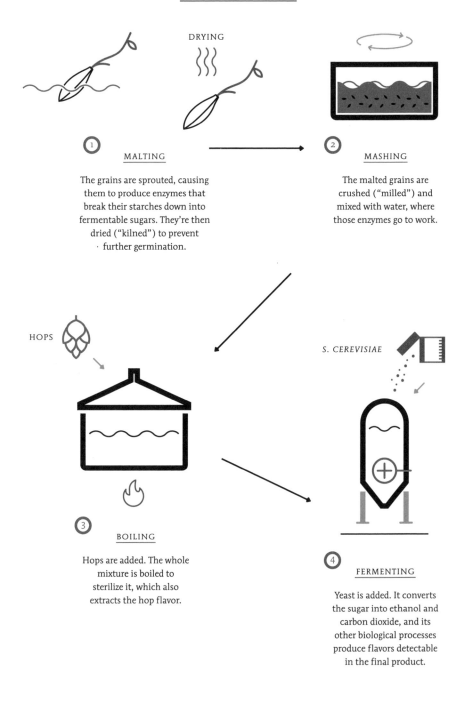

DRYING

1 MALTING

The grains are sprouted, causing them to produce enzymes that break their starches down into fermentable sugars. They're then dried ("kilned") to prevent · further germination.

2 MASHING

The malted grains are crushed ("milled") and mixed with water, where those enzymes go to work.

HOPS

3 BOILING

Hops are added. The whole mixture is boiled to sterilize it, which also extracts the hop flavor.

S. CEREVISIAE

4 FERMENTING

Yeast is added. It converts the sugar into ethanol and carbon dioxide, and its other biological processes produce flavors detectable in the final product.

Whether hopped beer tastes better than *gruitbier* is a matter of personal preference, but hops came to predominate because of their effectiveness as a preservative. Hops are a source of fairly potent antimicrobial chemicals that are easily extracted in ethanol. Two of them, humulone and lupulone, actually get their names from the hop plant, which is called *Humulus lupulus* in scientific parlance.

That natural preservation translated into a significantly longer shelf life for the medievals' beer, which didn't have the benefit of modern pasteurization and bottling techniques. Since then hops have become a part of the tradition and canon of beer.

We could absolutely make un-hopped beer today without fear of spoilage. A handful of producers have begun that very experiment, although they generally replace the hops with *gruit* or some other flavoring used in pre-hops recipes. After all, brewers have been flavoring their fermented barley for six thousand years. Why stop now?

Carbonation and Bottle Fermentation

Carbon dioxide gas gets into your glass or bottle in one of two ways. If you've read the section on yeast fermentation, this might seem strange. CO_2 is a product of fermentation—shouldn't that be an adequate source of carbon dioxide in your final beverage? Actually, the carbonation in your glass of bubbly isn't even from the initial fermentation. What happened to it?

Y
*Yeast Fermentation,
p. 20*

In short, it escaped. Not in the jailbreak sense, either—the brewer almost certainly allowed it to.

Fermentation produces a lot of gas, and, particularly for large operations, it's often not practical to try to retain that CO_2. Adding to the difficulty of preserving the original carbon dioxide gas is the fact that fermentation also produces a lot of heat, and gases don't like to stay dissolved in hot liquids. Imagine heating a pot of ginger ale on your stove and trying to keep it from going flat—doesn't sound so easy, does it?

Another challenge is the pressure. A hot, fermenting liquid that's producing a lot of hot, expanding gas will generate a lot of pressure. If you know any home brewers, there's a good chance you know someone who has tried to bottle beer that wasn't finished fermenting and wound up with a closet full of exploded bottles.

But you don't have to take their word or mine to know that fermentation can produce dangerously high pressures. The old United States Industrial Alcohol Company gave us plenty of evidence for this when their tank of partially fermented molasses burst its seams in 1919, flooding downtown Boston with two million gallons of the sweetener and killing more than twenty people.[1]

Getting back, then, to the safe methods of carbonating drinks: there are two. The more elegant one, used in Champagne production as well as bottle- and cask-conditioned beer, does actually use a fermentation process but not the same one that makes the booze in the first place.

After the primary fermentation is done and the product is otherwise ready, a secondary fermentation is initiated by the addition of a little bit of sugar, a little bit of yeast, or both. What happens next depends on the particular beverage being made.

Bottle-conditioned beers will undergo this second fermentation in the bottle (*conditioned* is simply beer jargon for "aged" or "matured"). These tend to improve as they age—a rare quality among beers—because the yeast continues to act on the flavor chemicals the beer contains.

Cask-conditioned beer, on the other hand, is put into a barrel for the second fermentation, which allows the yeast to interact with the flavor chemicals from the wood as well as those already in the beer. These beers are not subsequently bottled, so if you want to try one you'll have to order it at a bar or buy an entire cask yourself.

Some sparkling wines, such as the Italian prosecco, undergo secondary fermentation in a pressurized vat that keeps the carbon dioxide from escaping.

Champagne is a funny case. Its secondary fermentation takes place in a bottle, and it is aged in contact with the yeast, just like a bottle-conditioned beer. But there is an intermediate step before Champagne's final bottling, called "disgorging." When the sparkling wine has reached the desired age the yeast and sediment are carefully and quickly removed, with the help of the significant accumulated pressure in the bottle. The Champagne is then topped off with *liqueur d'expédition*, a mixture of sugar and reserved wine, and corked.

The bottles that contain sparkling wines and bottle-conditioned beers are unusually thick, and the corks are mushroom-shaped and held on with a wire basket. All of this is to protect against explosions. The pressure inside a bottle of Champagne is between four and six units of atmospheric pressure (depending on whom you ask), or about sixty to ninety pounds per square inch (psi). For reference, your car's tires are probably around thirty-two psi.

The second way carbon dioxide gets into your drink is by forced carbonation, which is exactly what it sounds like. Pressurized carbon dioxide gas is pumped into the liquid at a low enough temperature that it dissolves.

I realize those dancing bubbles in your bottle of beer may seem less magical now, so here's a fun tidbit that may make up for it: artificial carbonation of water was invented by Joseph Priestley way back in the 1770s. His experiments were possible because of the excess carbon dioxide gas produced at a nearby brewery; stimulating flat beer was one of the first uses Priestley proposed for his new method.

Filtration and Fining

If you've ever had a Belgian or Trappist beer, you may have seen sediment swirling at the bottom of the bottle. It's not a bad thing, but many people, understandably, find it unattractive.

So what is it? Leftover bits of grain? Something more sinister? Mercifully, no. It's yeast, sort of. Specifically, the sediment is a mixture of living and dead yeast cells and some of the heavier compounds they've created, all clumped together. Any fermentation will produce deposits like this eventually. Remember that fermentation is the work of a colony of microorganisms and that organisms tend to reproduce when they're happy. Yeast hanging out and fermenting up a storm will make more yeast. When there are enough of them, you'll be able to see the party.

But not every beer or wine has visible sediment. Brewers and vintners looking to create a clean and palatable product go out of their way to filter the beverages they make in a host of clever and bizarre ways.

Let's begin by talking about the production of "cold-filtered" or "cold-conditioned" beer. Although ubiquitous as marketing terms, these phrases do actually mean something.

The traditional technique for making lager beer involves keeping it at just above freezing for an extended period of time. If there is still yeast in the mixture, it will continue to work, and the carbon dioxide it produces will help to get rid of unwanted flavors. Even if there isn't leftover yeast, the cold will still cause some of the heavier things dissolved in the beer to clump together and precipitate out. Those who bother to observe a difference might call the method that uses yeast "cold conditioned" and the yeast-less one "cold filtered," but the terms have become largely interchangeable in practice.

Another option for removing sediment, called "fining," involves mixing in another substance that attracts the suspended particles to bind to it. This method is popular among winemakers and is also used in some beers.

Long organic molecules like proteins are most effective at fining, and egg whites, gelatin, casein, and isinglass (from the swim bladders of fish) have all been used historically, making many wines unfriendly to strict vegans. Some contemporary makers prefer bentonite clay or synthetic substances with similar characteristics.

In any case, there will be solids that still need to be removed, and this is generally done mechanically. One technique for eliminating the debris involves a filter made of diatomaceous earth, which is essentially fossilized algae. Beer or wine is poured through a bed of the stuff, which is porous enough to allow the liquid through but traps the solid particles behind.

Centrifuges are a popular alternative to filtration. This may strike you as incongruous, since they're most commonly associated with scientific and industrial applications, but then commercial fermentation is very much both.

Filtration and fining can cause producers a lot of headaches. There's no guarantee that only the bad things will be removed or that only the good ones will be left behind. Certain filters can impart flavors of their own. And the process usually requires additional exposure to the air, which increases the possibility that the brew will pick up unwanted microbes or that oxidation will change some of its flavors.[T]

And if wine is filtered and fined, what's that sediment in your dusty old bottle of red? Something the producers missed? Not quite. Over the years, the wine's tannins and other large, heavy molecules clump together and sink.

Y

Degradation of Spirits over Time, p. 65

Terroir

A well-used term in the wine industry, *terroir* refers to the effects of the land and location of production on the finished product. It's often applied to other products as well, from coffee to estate-produced spirits like *rhum agricole*. It's meant to indicate something special and distinctive about the product that can't be replicated by another maker somewhere else.

This is obviously good for marketing, but does terroir have a real effect? Tread cautiously, because we're about to enter a very heated argument in the world of wine.

First, there are a few things that absolutely do vary based on where a wine is produced. One of the most certain ones is the profile of wild yeast in the area. Even if the winemaker deliberately introduces a strain of *S. cerevisiae* to start the fermentation, the grapes will have some naturally occurring yeast and bacteria on their skins when they're crushed that will get in with the juice. Unless the juice is thoroughly sterilized, those microorganisms will play some role in the fermentation and contribute some set of flavor characteristics that a wine made somewhere else might not have.

Another factor in terroir is how conducive the soil is to growing the grapes. From the vine's perspective, mild temperatures and lots of water and nutrients are really great and conducive to growth. But we don't want to make wine out of the vine or the leaves, we want to make it out of the grapes, and the vine puts proportionally more energy into making those when its environment is difficult.

From the vintner's perspective, then, the goal is to give the vine all the resources it needs to be healthy, and absolutely nothing else. Well-drained soil, ideally on a hillside, can make this task much easier. So can a soil that is neither deficient in nutrients like nitrogen and potassium nor holding an excess of them.

What's still not settled about terroir is whether soil minerals make it into the fruit and through the fermentation process in a way that affects the wine's taste directly, or whether they contribute only indirectly by affecting the way the plant grows. Certain yeasts and bacteria are known to produce compounds with an earthy or mineral flavor, and it may be these that are responsible for the clay note of a Tuscan red or the flintiness of Chablis.

Certainly, though, there is something to the notion that a wine grown and made in a particular place can be in some way distinctive. In Spain, researchers produced two wines from theoretically identical vines grown sixteen hundred feet apart. The result? They had noticeably different flavors—one had raisin notes and a higher alcohol content and the other tasted more like apples—but no specific tastes could be attributed to the soil itself.[2]

Terroir is not generally considered as important in spirits made from molasses, cereal grains, or any commodity that is purchased on the open market rather than grown consistently in one location. But it's not in any way clear that terroir effects can't apply to products we think of as fungible.

The Bruichladdich Scotch Distillery is currently conducting an experiment in which it is making four different Scotches from barley sourced from four very different environments around Scotland. Meanwhile WhistlePig is trying out an estate whiskey made from rye grown on its farm in Vermont. We should have fairly strong evidence of terroir effects (or their absence) on beverages made from cereal grains within a few years.

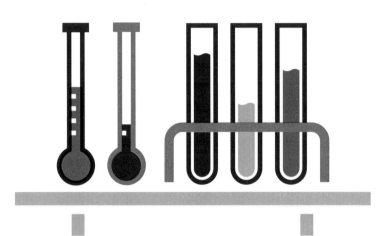

2. Distillation

What Is Distillation?

Fundamentally, distillation is the separation of a mixture's parts. This may be done to remove things that are not desirable (methanol from ethanol) or to concentrate things that are (ethanol at the expense of water), but it is always a separation of things that are already there. Unlike the fermentor, the still does not add anything beyond what the distiller puts in.

This separation is most often accomplished by heat distillation (although freeze distillation is discussed here as an alternative), which relies on the fact that different liquids boil at different temperatures.

Ethanol, for instance, boils at 173 degrees Fahrenheit, while water boils at 212 degrees. Because of the gap between their boiling points, we can separate a mixture of the two by heating it to 173 degrees, collecting the ethanol vapors, and allowing them to cool and recondense in another vessel, leaving the liquid water behind. This is the basic principle of most stills.

How Whiskey Is Made

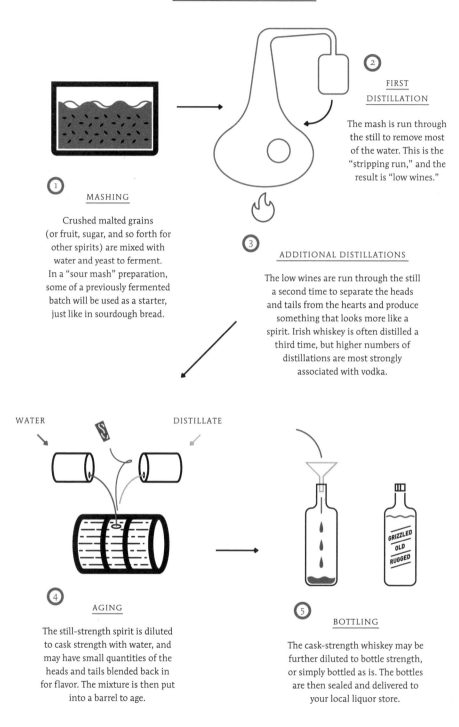

② FIRST DISTILLATION

The mash is run through the still to remove most of the water. This is the "stripping run," and the result is "low wines."

① MASHING

Crushed malted grains (or fruit, sugar, and so forth for other spirits) are mixed with water and yeast to ferment. In a "sour mash" preparation, some of a previously fermented batch will be used as a starter, just like in sourdough bread.

③ ADDITIONAL DISTILLATIONS

The low wines are run through the still a second time to separate the heads and tails from the hearts and produce something that looks more like a spirit. Irish whiskey is often distilled a third time, but higher numbers of distillations are most strongly associated with vodka.

WATER

DISTILLATE

④ AGING

The still-strength spirit is diluted to cask strength with water, and may have small quantities of the heads and tails blended back in for flavor. The mixture is then put into a barrel to age.

⑤ BOTTLING

The cask-strength whiskey may be further diluted to bottle strength, or simply bottled as is. The bottles are then sealed and delivered to your local liquor store.

GRIZZLED OLD RUGGED

Vapor pressure is one of the most important concepts to grasp if you want to understand how stills work. If you aren't familiar with it, or need to brush up, now would be a great time to turn to the Appendix for a summary.[T] A still is essentially the scientific concept of vapor pressure realized in the form of a tool.

Y
Vapor
Pressure and
Volatility,
p. 169

The Pot Still

A simple, old-fashioned pot still is basically a heated chamber, containing the mash, with a pipe (the neck) leading out of it to a condenser. Ordinarily, the top of the chamber has some kind of taper leading into the neck. This design makes it a bit easier for the vapors to escape the chamber—and not just the ones from the ethanol.

You can build a still at home, and many people do, although I should warn you that it's illegal to do so in the United States. In part that's because it's possible to blow yourself up, and it's very easy to poison yourself, if you don't know what you're doing.

A distillation run has three segments, known as the heads, the hearts, and the tails, which occur in that order.[TT] Pot stills aren't especially efficient, and they produce a "smearing" effect along the boundaries between these segments. That may not sound good, but it is. It's the reason that a spirit like whiskey retains its complexity after being boiled and separated—smearing between the segments leaves flavors in the distillate that we couldn't completely remove even if we wanted to.

YY
Heads
and Tails,
p. 45

As the temperature goes up during the distillation process, all the liquids in a particular mash will tend to vaporize at higher rates. Just because the still is heated to ethanol's boiling point doesn't mean there are no vapors from the water or heavier flavor chemicals. The percentage of each that makes it through at any given point depends on the still, and stills can be very idiosyncratic. Even the angle of the lyne arm (the connection between the neck and the condenser) will change the final result.[1]

The other side of that beautiful inefficiency is that it's hard to get everything you want in your spirit out of a single run. Many makers will send the spirit through once to remove water—it's a long way from 8 percent alcohol to eighty proof—and run the result, called a "low wine," through a second time to produce the final spirit. Some producers will add a third distillation run for even greater precision.

What comes out of the pot still in the end might be in the neighborhood of 170 proof—much higher and it would be impossible to keep those mysterious, delicate flavors in. This is why pot stills are normally used for spirits like Scotches and rums that live or die on their complexity, and why vodkas are generally prepared by column stills.

The Column Still

The column still is also called the "continuous still," because in principle you can run it indefinitely; a pot still is generally cleaned out between runs. The column still is designed to make the most of reflux, the process by which some of the vapors recondense and return to the liquid mash. Heavier substances are more likely to do this than lighter ones; this recondensing helps the distiller to separate the heads and tails of a run from its hearts.[T]

Y
*Heads
and Tails,
p. 45*

Reflux also occurs in pot stills, some of which have especially long necks or upward-angled lyne arms to facilitate the process. (The farther away the vapors get from the boiler, the cooler they become and the more likely they are to condense.)

But column stills take reflux to a whole different level, achieved by a series of bubble-cap plates or lightweight packing materials that act as condensation points along the way.

Vapors most easily condense back into liquids when they can latch onto something.[TT] A lot of things can serve as the nucleus for condensation, including bits of dust and droplets that have already formed (there's a good chance this type of condensation is happening in a cloud above you right now). Inside a still the

YY
*Beer Head,
p. 72*

Pot Still

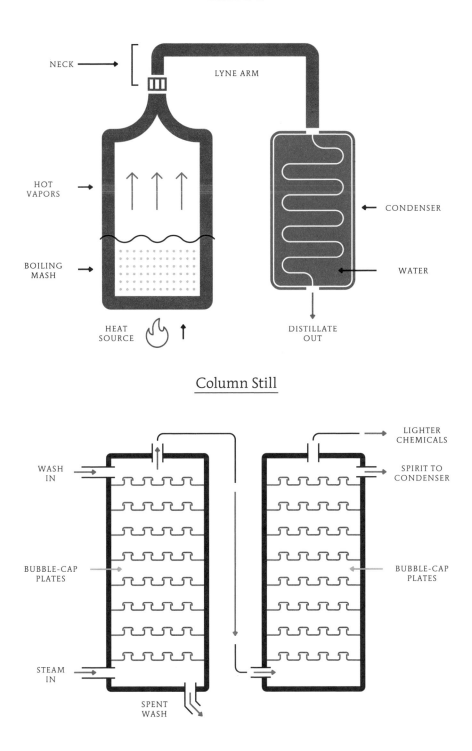

NECK

LYNE ARM

HOT
VAPORS

BOILING
MASH

HEAT
SOURCE

CONDENSER

WATER

DISTILLATE
OUT

Column Still

LIGHTER
CHEMICALS

WASH
IN

SPIRIT TO
CONDENSER

BUBBLE-CAP
PLATES

BUBBLE-CAP
PLATES

STEAM
IN

SPENT
WASH

vapor usually latches onto a solid surface. The structure of the continuous still is designed to provide as many solid surfaces as possible in order to maximize reflux.

This makes a column still so efficient that doing a single run is like doing a hundred runs through a pot still. It's very easy to get to 95 percent ethanol, which is about as high a concentration as one can get in practice—so easy you can do it by accident. That's great for making vodkas and gins, where the goal is to get to pure ethanol and water and then add flavors of your own. But any time you want to preserve the complexity of the fermented mash, using a column still is playing with fire. Major American whiskey producers use column stills the size of buildings; they can make them work because they have substantial industrial know-how. If you're trying to make whiskey at home (which, I feel obliged to remind you again, is illegal and might kill you), you'll be better off with an old-fashioned pot still.

Freeze Distillation

Pot stills and column stills both use heat to separate the components of the mixtures you put into them. Freeze distillation is the natural correlate of that process: liquids that boil at different temperatures also tend to freeze at different temperatures.

Water, for instance, freezes at thirty-two degrees Fahrenheit, a temperature easily reached in the winter in much of the temperate world. Ethanol, on the other hand, needs to get all the way down to –173 degrees Fahrenheit before it solidifies.

That means you can turn a solution of water and ethanol into pure ethanol by freezing the water out of the mixture. In Colonial America applejack was made by fermenting apple cider and leaving it outdoors in large vats when the weather got cold. Add a spigot at the bottom and *boom*: you've got apple moonshine, ready to serve.

I can't recommend this technique, as easy as it may sound, for the same reason it's not in use anymore: the water is basically the only thing freeze distillation removes. Any impurities that might be present at harmless levels in the cider (or beer, or wine, or whatever else you might care to distill) will be concentrated along with the ethanol. The poisonous alcohol methanol, for instance, doesn't freeze until about -144 degrees Fahrenheit. This is above ethanol's freezing point, sure, but not a temperature you're likely to encounter in your backyard.

Heads and Tails

Heads and *tails* (also known as *foreshots* and *feints*, respectively) are distillers' terms; they're contrasted with *hearts*, the portion of a distillation run that will make up the bulk of the finished spirit. I've used these words in the above descriptions of how stills operate and what they produce. Let's take a moment and explain what they really are.

The mash produced by fermentation is an extremely complex mixture containing an inconceivable number of distinct chemicals. Living things tend to be that way. The elements within that universe of organic matter span a whole range of weights and volatilities. Distillation pulls those substances apart in a broadly consistent order, starting with the lightest and most volatile first. These lightweight elements are the heads.

In this early part of the run you'll find some of the most delicate flavors. You'll also find things you definitely don't want to drink, like acetone and methanol. Heads are sometimes used to clean the stills because they contain fairly good solvents and they evaporate very easily, leaving minimal residue.

Tails are heavier substances that tend to be left behind when most of the ethanol has boiled off. They contain fusel alcohols— longer molecules similar to ethanol that can produce fruity flavors that may or may not be wanted—and some fatty acids. Generally, if a substance is big, it's in the tails.

Tails generally aren't poisonous, as heads can be. In fact, they're often blended back into the finished spirit to add flavor

What Comes Off the Still

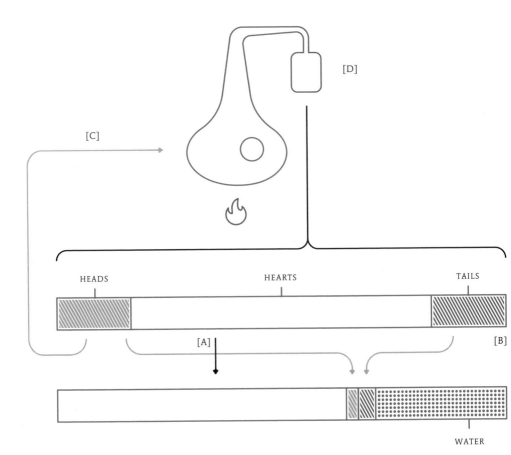

[A]
The hearts make up the bulk of the final spirit. Depending on the spirit, a portion of the heads, tails, or both may be blended back in before bottling.

[B]
Tails are often rich and flavorful. They may be added to future distillation runs, or collected until they can be distilled on their own, as in the case of "Queen's Share" rums.

[C]
Some distillers reuse a portion of the heads to clean their equipment. After all, the harshest elements of the heads are highly effective solvents that evaporate easily—what more could you ask for?

[D]
Spirits are usually distilled at least twice. In the first run, the goal is to strip out as much water as possible. In the second run, the distiller will make cuts between the heads, hearts, and tails of the distillate.

and complexity; this is especially likely if the liquor is going to be aged, because that process will help get rid of any off notes.[T]

In a way, you can think of the tails as the spirit equivalent of fat on a cut of meat. There's a proper balance that makes the whole thing magical. The ability to control that balance—by deciding how much of the heads and tails to blend back into the spirit—is one of the (many) fun parts of being a distiller.

[Y] What Is Aging?, p. 53

There's even a certain old-fashioned type of rum that is made specifically from the redistilled tails. It's called the Queen's Share, which should tell you a thing or two about how highly prized these flavors can be.

When distillation is finished, anything that isn't volatile is left behind. This includes all the pigments: what comes out of the still is always clear, regardless of what it looked like going in. If your spirit has color, it was acquired during the aging process or added artificially.

Methanol

Why can bathtub gin make you go blind? Methanol, chiefly.

This highly volatile alcohol is frequently used as an antifreeze, which you might recognize as something you shouldn't drink. Once inside your body, methanol is metabolized to formaldehyde, which you might recognize as something *else* you shouldn't drink. Formaldehyde is then metabolized into formic acid.

Methanol poisoning is the most common way that people find themselves with a toxic dose of formic acid in their blood. Its presence can cause metabolic acidosis, which is the technical term for your blood turning progressively more acidic. If that sounds horrifying, good—I'm doing my job.

Metabolic acidosis, induced by formic acid, can cause permanent damage to your optic nerves, which is the reason blindness is associated with poorly distilled spirits. If you get rid of the water but leave this stuff in, you'll get a buzz, sure, but it's not the good kind.

Distillation Flavor Wheel: White Rum

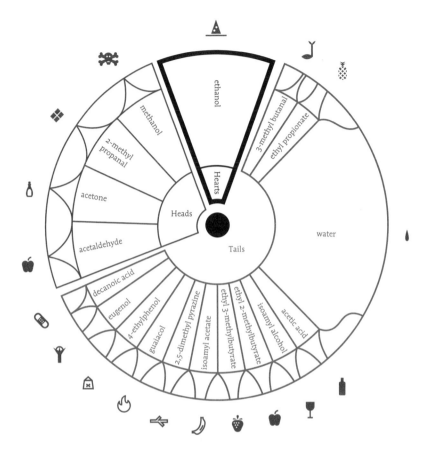

These flavors are arranged clockwise, in the approximate order in which they'd boil off in the still, beginning with acetaldehyde. Think of the line between the middle and exterior sections as the boiling point for each substance in turn: inside that line, it's at its full, pre-distillation concentration; beyond it, distillation and blending have brought the chemical to its final concentration.

Note that this image is not to scale (water would take up sixty percent of it if it were). The relative sizes of sections are meant to suggest differences in concentration, not to represent them precisely.

Also keep in mind that the clear boundaries shown between chemicals are just for convenience. In practice, you'll get a little bit of a lot of different things coming off the still at any given moment.

Flavors

Left unchecked, metabolic acidosis is a process that can shut down your kidneys, put you in a coma, or kill you outright. Which one happens depends on how much you've consumed and how quickly you're treated.

Remarkably, one of the most effective treatments for methanol ingestion is ethanol. Because the thing that does the most damage is the formic acid—a by-product of methanol metabolism—if you can find a way to stop the body's metabolism of methanol you can keep the patient alive. Alcohol dehydrogenase, the enzyme responsible for metabolizing alcohol in our bodies, will preferentially metabolize ethanol over methanol if given a choice. Administering ethanol means the methanol stays untouched, keeping the formaldehyde and formic acid from forming in your system, at least temporarily.

Methanol shows up in concentrations of a few dozen milligrams per liter in beer, upwards of a few hundred in wine, and more still in distilled spirits. Methanol occurs in fresh fruits and vegetables as well in varying concentrations—sometimes at as low a level as it is in beer, though sometimes there is twice as much as you would get in a glass of wine. Chances are there's even some in your saliva right now. In none of these cases is methanol going to kill you; you can metabolize about 1,500 milligrams in an hour without running into too much trouble, according to the Food and Drug Administration. Steer clear of the concentrated stuff from the moonshine still, and you should be just fine.

Filtration of Spirits

After being distilled, some spirits—I'm looking at you, vodka!— are put through a filtration process. Generally this means exposure to activated charcoal, which is used for its adsorbent properties. That's not a typo. *Absorption* involves one thing permeating another, root and branch; *adsorption* happens on the surface. Activated charcoal, for instance, has a lot of reaction points because it is processed, or activated, to have a very high surface area. It adsorbs chemicals from the liquid it's immersed in by attaching them to its outer surface.

Distillers filter their products to strip out impurities that remain after the *nth* distillation. It isn't clear how significant the effects are if the still is a good one, but if the goal is a neutral spirit it certainly can't hurt.

If you're wondering whether you can apply this principle at home to turn lower-quality bottled vodka into top-shelf stuff, a number of websites have published guides on the topic. It's not completely insane, although the difference it makes is probably overstated.

The good news is, while a large distiller may be able to get a higher-quality supply of activated charcoal or know how to use it better than you do, the science of putting vodka through a filter doesn't change when you're doing it in your kitchen instead of a commercial distillery. If the bottom-shelf vodka you have hasn't already been filtered, it will definitely do something.

Now, the bad news: activated charcoal doesn't catch everything. If the molecule doesn't react with carbon, it won't get filtered out. So if you're starting with a vodka that has been inexpertly distilled and has a lot of impurities that were left behind in the process, you can't be sure the filter will catch them all. And if your vodka is good enough that you don't have to worry about excessive impurities, I'm not sure why you would want to refilter it in the first place.

3. Aging

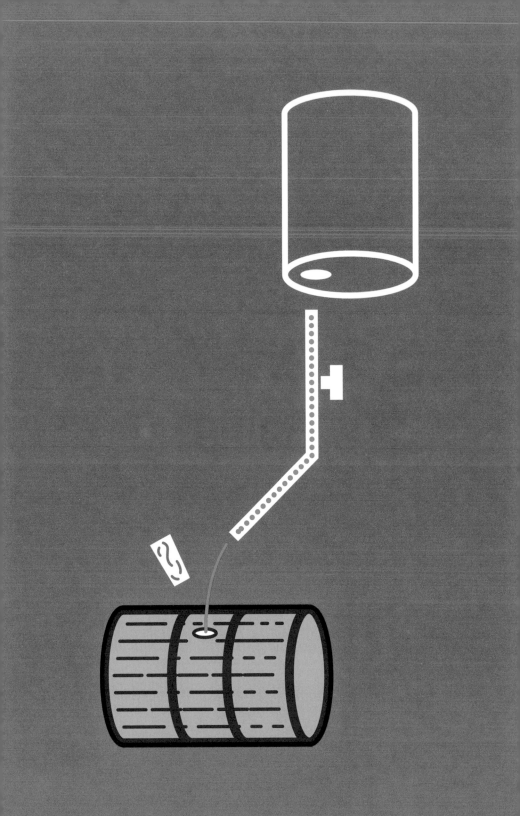

What Is Aging?

You've made your home brew, or your white lightning, and now you've got a choice: put it aside for months or years to age, or get out the cups and enjoy it now. Why would anyone ever pick the first one?

People often talk about aging as a way of smoothing out or softening the flavors in your drink. That sounds nice, but it's meaningless if you have no reference for the terms—and *smooth* isn't exactly a technical term in chemistry.

Aging, at its simplest, is changing the composition of flavor chemicals in your booze. The brew may lose ethanol and water, too, but if that were all aging did we'd have given it up a long time ago.

Aging is the part of the process during which brandy picks up its warm vanilla and caramel notes, red wine loses its tannic bite, and bourbon can pick up the slightest hint of sherry. It's all about patience and the subtle chemistry of taste.

Bottle Aging

How can something age in a sealed glass bottle? The barrel makes sense, sure—it's porous, it imparts a flavor of its own, and it lets the atmosphere in. But a bottle? Smooth, solid glass and airtight (unless you messed it up)—how can anything change in there?

A straightforward example of this kind of aging is bottle-conditioned beer, which is beer that continues to ferment in the bottle. There's some yeast and sugar in the beer when it's bottled, allowing it to get stronger and bubblier as the yeast turns sugar into ethanol and carbon dioxide.[Y]

Other microbes can also affect the bottle-aging process (deliberately or otherwise). Lambic beers—which, incidentally are often also bottle-conditioned—make use of bacteria to add sourness to the finished product. Stray cells of *Brettanomyces* can add a barnyard flavor to both lambic beers and wines, though it's usually undesirable in the latter case. *Acetobacter* can turn all that wonderful ethanol inside a bottle right into vinegar.[YY] Basically, if there are living organisms in the mixture when it's bottled, they'll go right on doing what they do as long as they can sustain themselves.

But you don't need bacteria or yeast to age something in a bottle. Even in the absence of a living agent, the oxygen contained in the small amount of air at the top can cause flavors to evolve over time by reacting with them. And the flavor chemicals present in the brew can also react with one another.

Let's look, for example, at red wine, and specifically its tannins, famous for their bitterness and their contribution to what the wine folks call "mouthfeel." Tannins are big and complex organic molecules. For comparison, water has a molecular weight of about eighteen grams per mole, while tannins can be one to two orders of magnitude larger than that.

The molecular size of tannins means that a lot can happen to them. Not only can they react with the acids and anthocyanins (pigments) naturally present in the wine, they can also break apart into other chemicals, "softening" the wine and improving

[Y] *Carbonation and Bottle Fermentation, p. 29*

[YY] *Other Fermenting Agents, p. 23*

its final taste. Bottle aging provides time for this to happen. Tannins also occur naturally in wood and can be absorbed into wine that's aging in a barrel—for aging to be really effective against tannins, the wine has to spend some time in a bottle.

It's easy to forget that beer—or wine or the spirit of your choice—is, at the chemical level, not one undifferentiated thing but a mixture of a vast number of substances capable of independent and ongoing reactions. This is especially true in fermented products, because fermentation is messy, hard to control, and largely out of our hands. There's always more going on than meets the eye.

Barrel Aging

This is more like it. When we think of aging, we think of rows of giant wooden casks filled with wine or whiskey. It's romantic, and it's generally still the right image, although some modern producers do age their spirits in stainless-steel vats, adding wood chips or used barrel staves for flavor.

Barrel aging started out as a storage method, advantageous because wooden barrels could be made watertight and were relatively durable. They've been used to transport wine and spirits for far longer than their effects have been understood.

Like the bottle,[Y] the barrel provides an environment in which the various flavor compounds can interact with one another and form new ones. The barrel can also bring into play three flavor-affecting elements not present in the bottle: the wood itself, the preparation applied to the wood, and the oxygen the wood allows in.

The barrels used for aging are generally made of oak.[YY] Oak, like all wood, is porous, which allows the aging liquid to move into and out of the walls of the barrel as it expands and contracts with fluctuations in temperature. Oakwood offers distinctive flavors for the liquid to absorb, including the vanilla-like vanillin so prized in bourbons and aged spirits generally.

Y

Bottle Aging, p. 54

YY

Woods Used in Cooperage, p. 57

Aging Flavor Chart

LEGEND: GAINED LOST

CHEMICALS →	FLAVORS		CHEMICALS →	FLAVORS
VANILLIN	VANILLA		DIMETHYL SULFIDE	FRUITY*
GUAIACOL	SMOKY		YELLOW PIGMENTS	N/A
4-METHYLGUAIACOL	SMOKY		BENZYL ALCOHOL	JASMIN/FORAL
EUGENOL	CLOVE		2-PHENYLETHANOL	ROSE
ISOEUGENOL	CARNATION/SPICY		ISOAMYL ALCOHOL	WINE/COGNAC
OAK LACTONES	OAK/COCONUT		GERANIOL	FLORAL
FURFURAL	NUTTY		LINALOOL	FRESH/FLORAL/WOODY
5-METHYLFURFURAL	CARAMEL		TARTRATES	CREAM OF TARTAR
WATER	(SOME)		TANNINS	BITTER/ASTRINGENT
ETHANOL	(SOME)		ANTHOCYANINS	N/A

*Dimethyl sulfide enhances fruity flavors in wine
up to a point, but in high quantities it just tastes like cabbage.

A wine or spirit will lose some flavors and gain others during the aging process.
In a bottle, these changes are due to interactions between the chemicals already present
when the bottle is sealed; the same reactions take place in a barrel, along with
evaporation, oxidation, and the introduction of some flavors from the wood.

In American whiskey production, a barrel's interior is generally charred before it's filled the first time. Just as wood has a set of flavors, so does the char; as combustion breaks down the structural elements of the wood, it produces chemicals that seem sweet, warm, and spicy. The resulting flavors are not that different from the ones you get when browning meat. This flavor profile, incidentally, is why it's far less common to age wine in a charred barrel.

The wood that will be made into wine barrel staves is ordinarily seasoned—that is, air-dried and exposed to the elements, as is done with firewood. This isn't done for flavor: dried wood is less friendly to microorganisms than freshly cut wood and therefore less susceptible to rot. But the process of seasoning also allows some of the long structural molecules in the wood to start to break down into smaller, more flavorful ones.

Oxygen, admitted through the porous wood (and in greater quantities after some of the liquid has evaporated), is the third critical element of barrel aging. Its presence substantially increases the variety of reactions that can take place in the liquid.

For example, the wood contributes a category of chemicals called aldehydes, which can react with oxygen to form carboxylic acids (stay with me). Those, in turn, can react with alcohols to form esters, which have fruity or floral flavors and wouldn't show up in the same concentrations without either the wood or the oxygen.

And all that is just the beginning—we have a long way to go before we scrape the bottom of this barrel (for anything but puns, that is).

Woods Used in Cooperage

Aging barrels are made of wood, and it's easy to imagine that the wood contributes a flavor of its own. Applewood- and hickory-smoked meats taste quite different, after all. So, how do you decide which wood to use to make your barrel?

Walnut, cherry, maple, and many other woods have been used for barrels at various points in history. Balsamic vinegar is traditionally aged in a series of casks made of several different kinds of wood, and there is a growing selection of craft spirits aged in barrels made from unorthodox woods. But overwhelmingly the barrels used to age wines and spirits are made of oak.

Oak heartwood is sturdy and full of interesting compounds. There are tannins, like those found in grape skins, seeds, and stems, which occur naturally to discourage pests from eating the wood; tannins absorbed during the aging process contribute to the astringency of the final product. There is also a suite of chemical compounds known as lactones that often have a woody, coconutty flavor; these are strongly associated with oak and are unimaginatively called the oak lactones. Other chemicals in the wood may give notes of peaches, tea leaves, or tobacco.

Then there are the wood's structural substances: lignin, cellulose, and hemicellulose. These are long molecules that aren't especially aromatic on their own, but when broken down by heating or microbial activity they can become quite tasty. Hemicellulose breaks down into sugars and gives off a toasted, caramel-like aroma. The breakdown of lignin produces a lot of vanillin, the distinctive compound in vanilla, which is one of oak's most prized contributions to aged spirits. American oak, in particular, tends to impart a lot of vanilla flavor. This makes it less than ideal for aging certain wines but an essential part of the American whiskey palate. Oak's distinctive flavor profile is also one of the reasons used bourbon barrels can find new life aging other spirits.[1]

Y
Finishing and
Barrel Reuse,
p. 61

Toasting and Charring

The wood that goes into a barrel has almost invariably been heated to some degree. The staves of a wine barrel may have been lightly toasted after seasoning but before being assembled;

Toasting and Charring

A layer of charcoal from toasting or charring the inside of the barrel acts as a filter, attracting undesirable flavors and drawing them out of the liquid.

With changes in temperature the spirit moves into the pores of the barrel wall, and back out again. During this process, the spirit extracts flavor from the wood and leaves some of its own flavor behind.

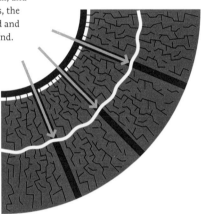

Barrel-aging gives spirits time to mature while gently exposing them to oxygen, evaporation, changes in pressure and temperature, and the influence of the wood.

the interior of an American whiskey barrel has probably been charred.

Heating wood breaks down the lignin, cellulose, and hemi-cellulose that form the structure of plant cells. These are long organic molecules, and when they're burned they break apart and release such flavor chemicals as smoky phenols, tobacco- and tea-like terpenes, and the signature lactones associated with oak, and whiskey, which have a slightly coconutty taste. These are all absorbed into the aging spirit from the wall of the barrel.

A heavy char is particularly associated with American whiskey. If you want to call your spirit bourbon, for instance, it has to be aged in charred new oak barrels, by order of the U.S. Alcohol and Tobacco Tax and Trade Bureau (TTB).[2]

When the practice of charring began in the nineteenth century it was done entirely to sterilize the inside of the barrel. Remember that barrels were just storage vessels at first—their flavor contributions weren't recognized until later, nor was the extra filtration that barrels provided, important though it is. As the liquid moves into and out of the wood, under changing pressure and temperature, the layer of what is essentially charcoal also acts as a mechanical filter, encouraging certain heavier elements to attach themselves to it and stay there.

All this adds up to a smoother spirit with a more complex flavor profile. Just remember that it takes time. Putting a lump of charcoal into a glass of vodka won't make it whiskey, however much you may want it to.

The Angels' Share

A barrel-aging term, the *angels' share* refers to the portion of the wine or spirit lost during the aging process. But "lost" is not a perfectly accurate description. Yes, in both wine and spirits the total amount of ethanol and water decreases. An aging spirit can lose 8 to 10 percent of its volume during its first year in a barrel, and it can be reduced by half if it's aged long enough. But in the process, the spirit's flavor is becoming more concentrated—far from losing anything, one could argue, the spirit is becoming more itself.

Most of the missing liquid is lost to evaporation. Barrels used for aging are watertight but not airtight, and some of this vapor will escape. In drier climates, relatively more water will evaporate; in wetter ones, relatively more ethanol will. You can often smell the booze getting away if there are enough barrels around.

The process of evaporation is helped by changes in temperature. When it's hotter, more of the liquid will vaporize, and the vapors will be under a higher pressure.[T] When it's cold, the vapors in the barrel will be under a lower pressure, which makes it easier for air to get in. Some ethanol is also lost during this process by reacting with oxygen, so the slow admission of outside air into the barrel over a long period of time is one of the reasons aging tends to smooth out strong wines and spirits.

Vapor Pressure and Volatility, p. 169

Angels' share is a very poetic name for this phenomenon, but the evaporating liquor will be consumed by something else long before it reaches the heavens. Ethanol is an energy source, after all, and the world is full of fungi and bacteria that can metabolize it.

Baudoinia compniacensis, for instance, loves the vapors. If you visit a distillery or an aging facility, there's a good chance you'll see some of it in the vicinity: a lichen-like matt of sooty blackness living on buildings, trees, fences, and whatever other surface it can find. It's not exactly pretty, and is annoying to property owners who want their surfaces clean, but otherwise these colonies are harmless—the fungal equivalent of, "Hey! I'm at this great new bar…"[3]

Finishing and Barrel Reuse

You've made your new oak barrel, charred it, and kept your bourbon in it for two years before bottling. Now you've got to get rid of that barrel—or at least you can't reuse it for your next batch of bourbon. The law says you need a fresh one. But don't worry: plenty of beer, Scotch, and even wine producers will be happy to take it off your hands.

But why do they want it? It isn't just that secondhand goods are cheaper.

Absorption is a two-way street. While your whiskey has been drinking in the barrel's flavors and filtering itself through the charcoal, it has also been leaving stuff behind. The used barrel can't impart as much of the wood's qualities to the next batch of whiskey as a fresh barrel might, but it can impart its absorbed flavors to something else, which a new barrel certainly cannot do (unless there's a whiskey tree out there and nobody's told me).

When you start making a spirit, in a way you've already set parameters that limit how it can ultimately taste. Your mash is set, as are your palette of microbes and your barrel; if you want a raisiny taste in your whiskey, for instance, you're going to have trouble getting it.[4]

Finishing gives you a way around this restriction. In this process, a wine, beer, or spirit that has been aged in its normal way is then transferred to a barrel that has previously been used to age something quite different—a Madeira wine barrel might be used to finish a whiskey, for instance—and kept there for the tail end of its maturation process. In a side-by-side comparison, you'd probably be able to pick out the beverage that had been finished in a used barrel, but it's unlikely that you'd be able to identify the barrel's previous occupant. Finishing is generally done in a limited way, in order to add flavor without changing the fundamental character of the product.

Sometimes used barrels are employed for the entire aging process. Ordinarily, barrels with strong flavors, like those that have held rum or port wine, aren't used for this kind of extended aging. Used barrels contribute some mellower notes borrowed from their prior contents, but the biggest advantage in using them is that their wood adds less of its own intrinsic flavor to the finished product.

New oak can be extremely pungent. Bourbon is aged in it for a minimum of two years, often more, but generally not for fifteen or twenty-five years. Scotch, which has a much higher median age, is almost invariably matured in used bourbon or sherry casks from the get-go.

A funny consequence of all this is that there is a robust international trade in empty barrels. At this very moment there may be a ship headed from a U.S. port to the United Kingdom laden with barrels that contain nothing but are insured for thousands of dollars.

Infusion

Jalapeño-infused bourbon. Dill-infused vodka. Basil-infused gin. Wherever you go, it's clear: infusion is having a major moment.

But what does it mean to infuse? Simply put, it's the process of extracting flavor from something by bringing it into contact with alcohol.

Plants produce flavor chemicals for a variety of reasons. Often they're meant to deter certain animals, such as insects, from eating the plant. If you've ever bitten into a peppercorn, you have a sense of how this works; the plants that we use as spices are generally in this category, which is why we use them in small doses.

Fruits, on the other hand, are full of flavor because they're hoping to be eaten. The apple doesn't fall far from the tree, as they say; if a tree is going to have healthy offspring that grow more than a few feet away, it helps to have its seeds carried off by animals enjoying the tasty fruit.[5]

While aroma compounds tend not to dissolve well in water, they're usually perfectly happy to do so in ethanol.[Y] This is why ethanol is a popular base for perfumes, and why adding theoretically tasteless vodka to your tomato sauce can change the flavor.

Y Ethanol as a Solvent, p. 171

Ethanol's status as a solvent is also why the world is full of flavored spirits. Liqueurs are traditionally made by infusing fruits and spices into neutral spirits (or whiskey, rum, or Cognac, in

Gin Flavorings

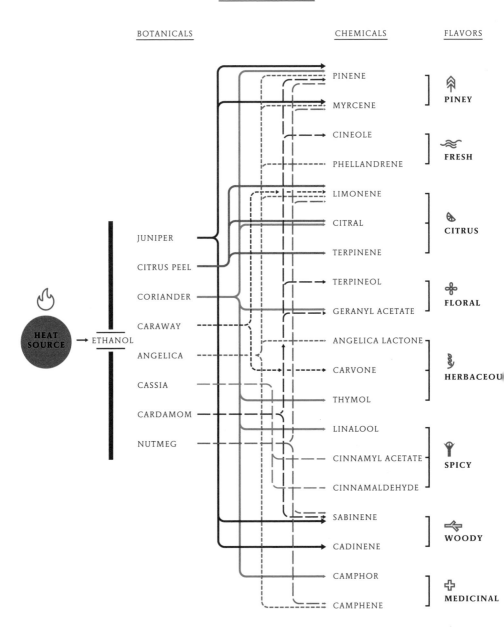

Gin can be made by infusing spices into neutral spirits, often followed by another distillation; or by hanging a basket of spices in the still itself, allowing the vapors to extract their essential oils. The particular spices used vary from gin to gin, in part because multiple spices can produce many of the spirit's flavors. Of the eight shown here, juniper is always present, by definition, while the other seven are relatively common inclusions.

some special cases). Gin, absinthe, and Scandinavian aquavit are often flavored by infusion and then redistilled to ensure that only particular aromas end up in the final product.

Infusion at home is incredibly easy. All you need is a jar or a bottle that you can seal, something aromatic, and your liquor of choice. It's easiest to start with fresh herbs, which tend to give off a lot of flavor very quickly, and to infuse them in a solution of vodka or grain alcohol. It's absolutely possible to use other liquors as a base, but that gets us into recipe territory, and there are other resources for that.[6]

Degradation of Spirits over Time

You may have come away from the section on bottle aging with a vague sense of foreboding.[T] If flavors can change in a sealed glass bottle, they can definitely change in an opened one, right? If that little bit of oxygen can age wine in a sealed bottle, what's all the air in a half-empty bottle of liquor doing to the spirit? Can flavors get worse over time?

Bottle Aging, p. 54

They can, and they do, I'm sorry to say. There are several mechanisms by which this happens.

The simplest one is evaporation. I don't mean losing ethanol, although if you leave your bottles uncorked, that'll happen, too. I'm talking about the lovely flavor chemicals in your spirit—the lightweight terpenes in your gin, for instance—which tend to dissipate over time.

Spirits are always releasing some of their flavor chemicals into the surrounding atmosphere. It's the only reason we can smell them in the first place: the evaporating molecules of a spirit actually get into our noses and make contact with receptors that can identify them. But this means that over time there are fewer and fewer molecules left to release.

Even more insidious is oxidation, which can both eliminate desirable flavors and turn them into foul-tasting ones. If you let your spirits make too much contact with the air, your gin's

Bottles Stored Under Different Conditions

An open bottle lets volatile aromatics out and oxygen in.

Visible and ultraviolet light can both break down long organic molecules, including the ones that give liquor its flavor.

Heat sources, including back-bar lights, promote evaporation and degradation of aromatics.

Keep your spirits sealed whenever you're not using them to prolong their shelf life.

Tinted glass and paper or wicker coverings are popular in the tropics to protect spirits from sunlight. These same techniques are often used with bitters, since it takes a very long time to finish a bottle.

Spirits stored in a cool, dark place are most immune to degradation—a great argument for an old-fashioned liquor cabinet.

citrusy limonene can turn into camphoraceous carvone, and your whiskey can pick up an *eau de* nail polish remover in the form of ethyl acetate. The ethanol itself can be oxidized into acetic acid, which is the distinctive flavor of vinegar.

There are other ways to abuse your liquor, too. As we've seen, flavor chemicals tend to be long organic molecules. Long molecules tend to break apart under certain conditions. If you keep your booze in a very hot environment or expose it to too much light (especially ultraviolet light), it will degrade much more rapidly, oxygen or no oxygen.

This is why Angostura bitters, for instance, is sold in heavily tinted bottles covered in paper. Bitters are used in drops and dashes; going through a whole bottle can take years. Angostura is doing what it can to keep its product fresh, regardless of how you store it. Rums intended for hot, sunny climates are often covered in wicker for the same reason.

Some bars and many nightclubs seem not to have gotten this memo. If you see a back bar with lots of cool lighting effects directed at the bottles, there's a good chance the spirits are being overheated and overexposed. Depending on what you're there for, this may not matter, but if you're looking for a fine old Scotch or aged rum you probably don't want the one that's been sitting on top of a light bulb.

As for your home bar, there are a few things you can do to help yourself and your spirits. One is to keep your stash away from windows and heating elements, preferably someplace dark. There's a very strong case to be made for a good old-fashioned liquor cabinet, especially for storing high-quality spirits that you might want to hang onto for a while.

But the simplest thing you can do is to drink your spirits when they're getting low. A half-empty bottle contains more air, and has a greater area of liquor exposed to that air—subject to higher oxidation and evaporation rates—than a nearly full one does. If you've had it for a while, your liquor has also had more time to be exposed to the harmful effects of heat and light. All these things are cumulative, so the second half of that bottle will degrade more perceptibly than the first half did, assuming you go through it at the same speed.

How much will this matter in practice? Probably not much, for the most part. That bottle of nice bourbon you opened a few months ago should still be very tasty. But if you've got a few nearly empty bottles lying around that you've had for years, use them as an excuse to clean house and throw a party.

4. Preparation

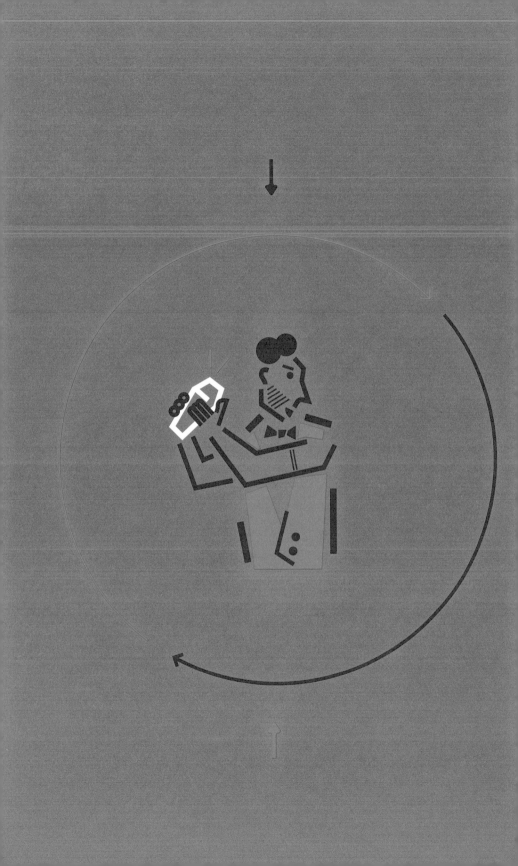

We are close—so agonizingly close!—to that first wonderful sip. But we still have more to cover, if we're not drinking straight out of the barrel or the still.

The preceding three chapters have covered the beauty of alcohol production, and the following three will deal with the mysteries of alcohol's effects on the human body. This chapter is the only place where we'll get to talk about the magic that happens at the bar.

Every drink is touched to a certain extent by the way it's consumed. This is most true of cocktails, in which the spirits are mixed with juices, wines, or one another—and sometimes with some violently attacked plants—and then chilled, diluted, possibly aerated, and served in a carefully selected glass. But beer, wine, and straight spirits are also affected by many of the same things: temperature, the presence of air or water, and even how they're presented.

So the next time you're savoring those sweet moments of anticipation between selecting a drink and tasting it, take a moment to appreciate how much the preparation will play into your drinking experience.

Beer Head

A hearty beer, perfectly poured, with a rich head of foam—it's one of life's great joys. But why does that foam layer form, and how? Believe it or not, scientists have carefully investigated this topic.

There are two important pieces to the beer head puzzle. Let's start with carbon dioxide. Beer contains dissolved CO_2, which usually has some desire to escape from the solution in which it finds itself. As it makes its getaway, the carbon dioxide forms bubbles of gas in the liquid. I feel very confident in assuming you've noticed these.

But the gas doesn't just get out on its own. It needs a rallying point, something to latch onto in order to form into a bubble. The technical term for this process is *nucleation*; if that sounds highly scientific, be assured it is. Nucleation in beer has been extensively studied by professional chemists and physicists.

Any surface that appears smooth to the naked eye will look rougher at the microscopic level. Your glass of beer, for instance, has small cracks and divots too tiny for you to see. These spots serve as nuclei on which the carbon dioxide gas collects and forms bubbles. You've probably noticed that bubbles tend to form and rise from a handful of discrete locations, and not equally throughout the glass or at random (ditto for the bubbles in a boiling pot of water). If you've seen this, congratulations: you've found the roughest points on the liquid's surface.

The bubbles themselves also serve as nuclei—that is, they attract more gas as they form and rise—just as anything jutting into the liquid tends to. The same concept explains why your soda fizzes when you add ice to it and why bubbles collect on your

Beer Head

Beer bubbles form at nucleation sites—the locations where a liquid is interrupted by another surface. Dissolved carbon dioxide will latch onto that surface and escape as gas.

The bubbles themselves also act as nucleation sites, attracting more carbon dioxide as they rise, causing them to expand. A filmy layer of proteins at the surface of the beer then traps the bubbles, forming foam.

If you pour your beer down the side of the glass, it flows smoothly and the dissolved gas encounters relatively few nucleation sites. If you pour it directly into the center of the glass, the liquid will be interrupted in a greater number of places, increasing the likelihood of bubble formation and creating much more foam.

straw: anything that isn't the solution or dissolved in it tends to attract the gas to its surface. The amplifying power of these attractions means that those little bubbles forming at the bottom of your beer glass can double in size by the time they reach the top.[1]

Once they get there, the bubbles collect and form a foam instead of evaporating right away. Think about other bubbles you're familiar with to understand why: soap bubbles, for instance, have an oily outer layer protecting the gas from dissipating or being absorbed back into the water.

In beer that oily layer consists of naturally occurring organic molecules (or, occasionally, commercially added substances designed for this purpose). The foam is therefore a mixture mostly of carbon dioxide and these proteins, which give it its structural integrity and cause it to have a slightly different flavor from the rest of the beer. These proteins are often left over from the initial grain mash; barley and wheat are especially strong contributors. Some of the proteins are flavor compounds added by the hops, which is one reason the foam can taste bitterer than the rest of the beer.

So why does pouring down the side of the glass render all this complicated foam formation moot? Because the gas stays dissolved in what is basically just a flowing liquid. If you want to un-dissolve the CO_2, your best bet is to introduce some turbulence—say, by letting the beer fall some distance and smash into the bottom of the glass or by shaking (or hitting) the bottle before you open it. The components of the foam are in there either way; it's just a question of whether you bring them together or not.

If you want to test this, try pouring your beer foamlessly down the side of the glass, and then stirring or swirling it vigorously. You'll see the head show up, clear as day.

Adding Water to Spirits and Cocktails

We think of stirring or shaking a cocktail as a chilling process, and it nearly always is. But in order to chill something with ice you have to melt the ice, and if it's a drink you're chilling, that means more water gets into it.

It would be easy to write this dilution off as an evil, imposed on us by the tyranny of ice cubes and easily dispensed with in post-refrigeration mixology. But, like many things in the world of booze, this accident proves to be a happy one. After all, we often add water to aged spirits served neat—a little splash can do quite a lot.

Remember that not everything that dissolves in ethanol will dissolve as easily in water, and vice versa. Chemicals that favor one over the other can dissolve in a mixture of the two to a certain degree but may not be fully happy about it. In some situations they will clump together to avoid the solvent they don't like.[T] Changing the balance of the drink with a splash of water will make some of these compounds more willing to disperse throughout the solution and encourage others to retreat into themselves.

Emulsions: Absinthe and Milk Punch, p. 85

Adding water can have clumping and dispersing effects with any spirit, but barrel-aged ones are affected in another way that's even more interesting. Whiskeys, brandies—really anything that's spent a long time exposed to oak—will contain some large molecules derived from the wood. These molecules have a tendency to collect at the surface of the spirit, inhibiting the release of other aromatics. Adding a splash of water breaks up the party and frees the volatiles. On top of all that, mixing water with ethanol generates heat, which tends to stimulate the release of volatile aromatics even more.[2]

Adding water also has the obvious but still important effect of reducing the proof of a given sip. The flavor of pure ethanol is distracting if there's too much of it. A research paper printed in no less a publication than the *Journal of the Institute of Brewing*

Decanting and Adding Water

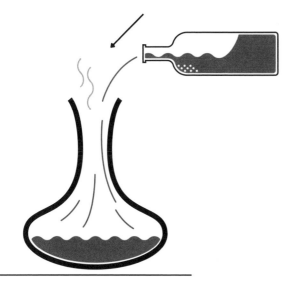

DECANTING

Wine poured into a decanter is rapidly aerated, resulting in the oxidation of some unwanted flavors. Decanting also provides an opportunity to separate the wine from its sediment, which remains in the bottle, and to present the wine in a more attractive vessel.

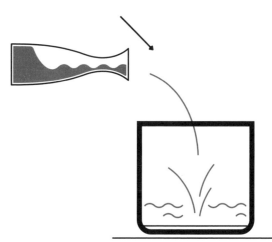

ADDING WATER

Adding water affects the solubility of some aromatic chemicals in hard liquors and increases volatility by generating heat. Certain large molecules can also collect on the liquid's surface, trapping desirable aromas beneath them, until dispersed by a splash of water.

recommends diluting Scotch to 20 percent alcohol by volume (ABV) for ideal nosing—that is, getting the most out of smelling your whiskey.[3]

Decanting and Shaking:
Aeration in Wine and Cocktails

Picture these two scenarios: the bottle of fine, aged red wine being poured gently down the sides of a crystal decanter; and the professional bartender, shaking a classic cocktail in a frosty, chrome-colored bullet. Romantic images, both. Even if these actions did nothing at all, the ritual would still have value.

Fortunately, we don't have to fall back on romance. Let's start with the simple explanation for each phenomenon.

Wine, in particular very old red wine, will often have sediment in it, built up as heavier substances clump together over time.[T] Simply pouring the wine into a new vessel gives you an opportunity to separate most of the liquid from the sediment at the bottom (and you're given a second chance when pouring from decanter to glass, if you let some through the first time). Most people prefer their wine without little bits of anything in it, so this is a very desirable step. Plus, decanters can be highly distinctive and even artistic, while wine bottles are generally all of a type.

Filtration and Fining, p. 31

Cocktail shaking, meanwhile, does the important task of mixing together ingredients that might be very heavy or even solid. If you've ever tried adding honey or granulated sugar to water, you've probably noticed that it doesn't instantly dissolve and distribute itself uniformly throughout the liquid. Heat tends to help things mix, as does vigorous agitation—and what could be more agitating than bouncing around in a metal tube getting hit with ice cubes along the way?

But what these two seemingly disparate processes have in common is aeration. Shaking a cocktail distributes the ingredients evenly, chills them, and adds water and air; while decanting a wine, swirling it in a glass, or simply leaving an open bottle of it out to "breathe" increases its exposure to the atmosphere.

Why on earth do we do this, when we've been so careful to protect our spirits from the air's effects?[T] Air, and oxygen in particular, can certainly do bad things to your booze. But a little can be very helpful.

Y
Degradation of Spirits over Time, p. 65

Young wines, for example, are often decanted as well as old ones, in the hope that the rapid oxidation will effect a desirable change in flavor. A team in China studied twenty components of red wine and found that the levels of most organic acids (things like tartaric and malic acid) and polyphenols (a big category—everything from tannins to pigments) were lower in wine that had been decanted.[4]

Meanwhile, the *act* of introducing air—that is, of exposing more of the wine or spirit directly to the environment—aids in the volatilization of aromatic compounds. These guys like to waft off into the atmosphere, which isn't nearly as easy when there's a lot of other liquid in the way; and if the aromatic compounds don't get into the air somehow, they can't make it to your nose. More surface area means more chances for these chemicals to volatilize.

If you'd like to test this principle at home, you easily can. Put an equal amount of water into two glasses, then pour one of them out on the counter. The puddle has greater air exposure, and should evaporate much more rapidly than the water in the remaining glass. The volatilization of aromatic chemicals is just a particular form of evaporation; a greater surface area exposed to the air increases the opportunities for those chemicals to turn into vapor, just like it does with water.

YY
Ice and Temperature, p. 81

Shaking also chills a drink, of course, but we'll explore that later.[TT] For now, know that vigorous aeration leads to dissolved gases in the liquid, which can lead to foam formation, especially if there are viscous ingredients in the mixture (a foam is basically a lot of bubbles suspended in a liquid; if that liquid is heavy enough, the bubbles have a tougher time escaping). It's conceivable that all that dissolved air has an effect on the taste, too, but as of this moment we don't have hard proof. Fortunately, the finest minds in the cocktail-science world are working on getting it as we speak.

Egg Cocktails

Many people blanch at the thought of a raw egg in their drinks. Surely it's unsafe! There's a reason we normally eat eggs cooked, right? And what could even be the point?

Let's take these objections one at a time. First, the safety. (My lawyer, my publisher, and my doctor have all politely asked me to remind you at this juncture that I am not a medical professional.) There's a very good chance you've eaten raw eggs already, in hollandaise sauce, mousse, or raw cookie dough, among many other examples. If you like eggs at breakfast but don't take them hard boiled, scrambled until very firm, or fried over hard, you've eaten an egg yolk that was below the USDA's standards for *Salmonella*-killing doneness.

And, if you're reading this, none of those things has killed you. The truth is, despite widespread unease, the occasional recall, and an admittedly nontrivial number of infections per year, most eggs are not infected with *Salmonella*. The FDA requires large producers to take certain steps to avoid contamination, and all USDA-graded eggs have gone through a sterilizing wash before packaging to eliminate bacteria on the shells, which is where *Salmonella* tends to congregate. In short, raw eggs should scare you way less than getting into your car (particularly once you add alcohol to either).[5]

But why add raw egg to a cocktail? The short answer is texture: drinks are most likely to call for egg whites, which impart relatively little flavor but lots of froth.

Eggs are dense in long organic molecules like fats and proteins, which can impart a thicker, creamier mouthfeel to a drink.[T] Eggs, especially the whites, which contain almost no fats, also provide

Texture and Mouthfeel, p. 97

Shaking a Cocktail

Dry Shake

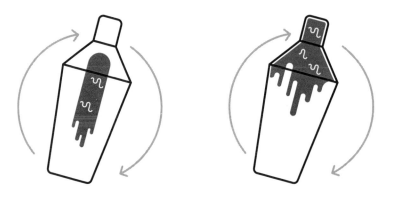

A dry shake involves shaking the ingredients of the cocktail without ice cubes. It's used primarily in egg cocktails, to give the eggs a chance to unfold their proteins (which they're less inclined to do when cold).

Wet Shake

A wet shake involves shaking the ingredients with ice cubes. Non-egg cocktails are basically always given a wet shake, and egg cocktails are usually given a wet shake after an initial dry shake. In either case, shaking helps distribute thick ingredients completely throughout the drink, while chilling and diluting it very rapidly.

structure. Shaking egg whites generates foam by introducing air bubbles and coating them with a protective layer of protein; this is the same reason it's possible to whip egg whites into a meringue. In shaken cocktails, acids and sugars help to stabilize the resulting frothy mixture—another reason to be grateful for the citrus and sweet things that go into a lot of these drinks.

Y

Beer Head, p. 72

An initial "dry shake" is often recommended for frothing cocktails that contain egg whites. That simply means shaking all the ingredients without ice to unfold the proteins, disperse the egg white throughout the mixture, and generate the foam; this is much easier to accomplish at room temperature than when the chilling has begun.

The drink is then cooled and diluted by means of a "wet shake," in which ice is used. Note that, because egg yolks are mostly fat, and fats and proteins respond differently to temperature, the dry shake ceases to be advantageous in whole-egg drinks—so if you ever want to make a batch of homemade eggnog, don't worry about shaking it twice.

One other interesting feature of eggs is their tendency to absorb certain aromatics. The same property that makes them an effective fining agent in wine[YY] means they can pull certain particles, like the oak tannins in a Whiskey Sour, to themselves preferentially. Because of this you may find that the foamiest part of your egg-based cocktail—like the head on your beer—tastes a little different from the rest.[YYY]

YY

Filtration and Fining, p. 31

YYY

Beer Head, p. 72

Ice and Temperature

If you're shaking, stirring, or simply serving on the rocks, you'll have to worry about ice at some point. There are reasons we prefer drinks at certain temperatures; here let's discuss how to get them there.[YYYY]

Heat tends to flow from your drink into the ice cubes. That heat can increase the temperature of the ice or change its state—from solid to liquid, say—depending on what else is going on.

YYYY

Effects of Temperature on Perception, p. 104

In practice, your drink will reach thirty-two degrees Fahrenheit before all the ice has melted, but the cubes will keep on sucking heat out of the liquid as they melt (albeit at a much slower rate). In other words, ice at thirty-two degrees tends to chill a drink to somewhere below thirty-two degrees, often as low as twenty-one degrees.[6]

It's amazing, the extent to which cocktail ice has been studied, fairly scientifically, by industry professionals. Thanks to their diligence I can tell you, for instance, that you hit diminishing returns on both chilling and dilution after about twelve seconds of shaking, regardless of the type of ice you use or how vigorously you attack the shaker. I can also confirm that stirring a cocktail will eventually chill and dilute it as much as shaking it will, but that, in practice, stirred drinks usually come out warmer and stronger.[7]

The most important lesson I can teach, taken from cocktail-science guru Dave Arnold, is probably that a stationary drink can cool only so fast. The thirty-two-degree meltwater that stirring or shaking will spread throughout the spirit or the cocktail, and the corresponding movement of fresh liquid to the surface of the ice cube, will bring your drink's temperature down a lot faster than just plopping in one big cube and waiting.

In short, if you want your drink really cold and diluted, shake it; if you're looking for somewhat cold and diluted, stir it; and if you're interested in making your drink only slightly cold and diluted, a single large ice cube is your best bet.

One other important lesson is that whenever possible you should use ice that has been held at thirty-two degrees. If your ice is colder than that it'll actually chill your drink less effectively, because more of the heat will go toward raising the temperature of the ice. If it has been kept in a warmer environment—say, sitting out in an ice bucket—the surfaces of the cubes will be coated in water, and for the same degree of chilling the ice will dilute your drink more. This problem becomes exacerbated the more surface area you're dealing with, making crushed ice a particular danger if it has been sitting out. On the other hand, a major advantage of fresh-cracked ice is in the low quantity of surface water compared to its surface area. This is why you often see it used at craft cocktail bars—well, that and its contribution to presentation.[8]

Bruising, Muddling, and Expressing

Ah, the mojito. An interesting highball popular at tropical resorts and among people who want to make a bartender miserable at eleven o'clock on a Saturday night. It's a particular flavor of labor-intensive, requiring the distinctive, elegant violence of the muddler. Why do we attack our fruits and herbs like this? And if it's worthwhile, why don't we do it in every drink?

Many plants collect their flavor chemicals in discrete areas. Very often these areas serve solely to encourage or deter animal feeding based on taste. Even flavors that we find pleasant can be meant as deterrents; as tasty as a few mint leaves are in a drink, you or any other animal are unlikely to eat an entire bed of them.

When those storehouses of flavor occur in leaves, they generally take the form of glands on the surface or somewhere in the interior. These glands secrete some of their signature scents naturally, which is why oregano smells like oregano. But if you want to release all of those chemicals, you need to break open the glands. Mastication accomplishes this; in cocktails, we do it by bruising or muddling the leaves.

Bruising is just about releasing a plant's aromatic oils. It's particularly useful with members of the mint family, which tend to have their glands on the leaf exterior. Muddling, on the other hand, tends to break open the leaf at a more structural level, which can be helpful with herbs like parsley that have their aromatic glands buried inside. Crushing the leaves, however, also releases all the other chemicals in the cells you're breaking up, including enzymes that can oxidize desirable flavors.[9]

Crushing Mint Leaves

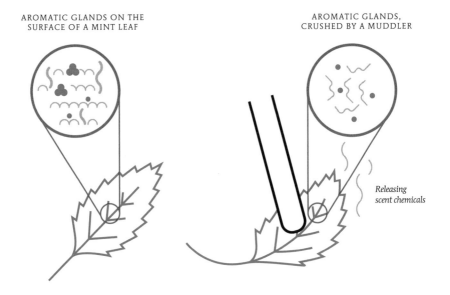

AROMATIC GLANDS ON THE
SURFACE OF A MINT LEAF

AROMATIC GLANDS,
CRUSHED BY A MUDDLER

*Releasing
scent chemicals*

Herbs contain glands full of
aromatic chemicals, sometimes
inside the leaves, and
sometime on the surface.
Ordinarily their contents are
released a little at a time.

Bruising or crushing a mint leaf
breaks open these glands,
releasing the aromatics all at
once. The same principle applies
to anything with a storehouse of
scent chemicals—citrus peels,
for instance.

It's not just leaves that get this treatment: we muddle citrus rinds as well, to release oils that don't necessarily make it out in the juicing process. Some people advocate for hand-squeezed citrus juice, on the grounds that it accomplishes the goal of extracting flavors more completely.[10]

Likewise, twisting—"expressing" is the technical term—a bit of lemon or orange peel over a cocktail does something to a drink's flavor. The action breaks open the aroma glands in the rind and releases a fine mist of flavorful oils over the drink, which you can generally see if you're paying attention.

Expressing a citrus peel adds one more fun option to the mix: flaming. Those oils spraying off your orange peel are combustible, and if you hold a lit match between the peel and the drink, you'll see a burst of flame during the expression. It's an awesome visual, and the drink ends up with both a bit of citrus and some of the toasty flavors that fire normally provides.⊤

Y
Toasting and Charring, p. 58

Emulsions: Absinthe and Milk Punch

The traditional preparation of absinthe is certainly dramatic. After you've poured your absinthe you're supposed to set a highly decorative slotted spoon on top of the glass, put a sugar cube on it, and then gently drizzle water down through the whole business. The technique is more art than science, but it produces a very well-known reaction: as the water drips in, the absinthe turns cloudy. Often called the "ouzo effect" because it also occurs in Greece's national spirit, this reaction is a consequence of the signature taste both beverages share and of the chemistry of emulsions.

Simply put, an emulsion is a mixture of liquids that normally do not mix. One of them is "dispersed," the other "continuous"— for our purposes, think of it as one liquid dissolved in another. Usually, emulsions take effort to make and maintain. A simple vinaigrette is a very common example: shake it up and you have

The Absinthe Effect

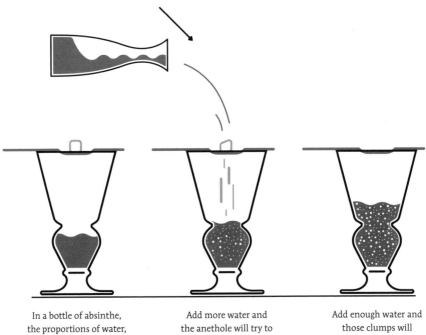

In a bottle of absinthe,
the proportions of water,
ethanol, and anethole
are in equilibrium.

Add more water and
the anethole will try to
get away from it, forming
clumps with other
like-minded molecules.

Add enough water and
those clumps will
become big enough
to scatter light and make
the drink look cloudy.

Like all anise-flavored spirits, absinthe contains anethole, a licorice flavored chemical
that doesn't dissolve as well in water as it does in alcohol. Anethole is responsible
for the clouding effect, or louche, for which absinthe and ouzo are particularly famous.

a fairly even mixture of oil and vinegar, but it will invariably need to be shaken again the next time you want to use it.

In both absinthe and ouzo a chemical called anethol (and specifically its trans isomer) is the important feature of our emulsion. It's the chemical that gives anise, fennel, and all related derivations their distinctive flavor. If, like me, you just don't like that licorice taste, it's anethol you don't like.

What anethol doesn't like is water. It hates dissolving in it, although it has no problem cozying up to ethanol. The bottle of absinthe you get at the store has an anethol-ethanol-water balance that keeps everything nicely mixed together. Add more water to your spirit and the balance gets thrown off; some of the anethol wants to un-dissolve and, once it does, it congregates in little clumps. These clumps get big enough to scatter incoming light, giving the absinthe its cloudy look.

Because it's the essential flavor of the liquor, there's really no way around anethol's visual effects—though cloudy absinthe appears to be less sensitive to light-induced degradation than the unwatered stuff, so you may not want to avoid it anyhow.[1]

Milk is also an emulsion, of milk fat in water. Proteins are suspended in there as well, specifically caseins. Caseins are amphiphilic—they form little clumps, called micelles, in the presence of water.

Degradation of Spirits over Time, p. 65

The clumps are small in regular milk, because their outer surfaces are all negatively charged and repel one another. But if you add an acid to the mixture, it tends to shed positive ions, which react with the micelles' surfaces and neutralize them. Now instead of being repelled from one another they can form larger, visible clumps, also known as curds.

In a milk punch, you want to hold onto the lactose—which is a sugar—and the subtle flavors of the milk but lose the thick proteins. So you'll want to add an acid to strip these out, such as citric acid (which you'll find in lemon juice), acetic acid (vinegar), or tartaric acid (cream of tartar). Then you can strain off the solids and enjoy what's left behind.

In spoiled (or fermented) milk, the sugar lactose has converted into lactic acid, which has the same effect. Though in that situation, straining the milk will not render it healthy or palatable.

Glassware

Which glass you serve your drink in has a ton of subtle effects, many of them aesthetic, associative, or psychological.^Y A few of the effects are physical, and they mostly have to do with the related concepts of temperature and volatility.

Remember that aromatic compounds have some tendency to waft off the surface of your drink. This needs to happen for you to smell them, but it also means that the contents of the glass are slowly becoming less flavorful.

A greater surface area tends to increase the rate of release from the drink into the atmosphere. You get a lot of aroma from a cocktail glass relative to its volume, because of the conical shape and broad mouth; a cylindrical rocks glass containing the same volume of liquid usually has less of it exposed to the air. This relationship between surface area and release rate holds for carbon dioxide gas as well, which is one reason that tall flutes have gained popularity over wider coupes for serving Champagne.

This effect can be compounded a bit by the shape of the glass above the fill line. Brandy snifters have a lot of headspace and a narrow opening; they're designed to maximize the release of aromatics from the spirit and minimize their ability to escape into the air, concentrating the smell right at your nose. Wine glasses also taper, if a bit less dramatically, for the same reason. If you've ever been told to pour wine to the widest point in the glass and no higher, this is why: more exposed surface area allows more of the flavors to come out to play.^{YY}

Another aspect of glassware choice has to do with drink temperature, which affects taste perception in a variety of ways.^{YYY} Warming a drink increases aromatic volatility. The snifter has a very short stem, because you're supposed to hold the bowl in your

---

Y
Psychological Influences on Intoxication, p. 121,
Psychological Influences on Consumption, p. 123

YY
Decanting and Shaking: Aeration in Wine and Cocktails, p. 77

YYY
Effects of Temperature on Perception, p. 104

Cups and Glasses

1 CHAMPAGNE FLUTE
- Narrow profile helps retain carbonation
- Height maximizes the visual effect of the bubbles

2 COCKTAIL GLASS
- Long stem lets the bowl stay cool, out of contact with the hand
- At a few ounces, just enough volume for a spirit-heavy cocktail

3 SNIFTER
- Bowl is warmed by contact with hand, releasing flavor chemicals
- Small opening concentrates aromas at the nose during the sip

4 JULEP CUP
- Made of silver or copper for thermal conductivity
- Chills the drink rapidly and reduces the ice's melting rate

hand, warming its contents and facilitating a consistent release of aroma (those brandy drinkers want to smell *everything*). Wine glasses, coupes, and cocktail glasses, all of which have longer stems, are designed to keep the bowl out of your hand, so you don't have to worry about temperature effects.

There are other things to consider when picking a glass as well. If you're filling it with ice, you don't want your glass to have a small bowl or a high center of gravity, which is why rocks glasses don't have stems. Julep cups are made out of thermally conductive copper or silver so that they turn frosty cold really fast and the crushed ice doesn't melt into the whiskey too quickly; the Mint Julep is ordinarily much smaller than its glass, after all, and its most important olfactory element usually comes from the garnish perched on top.[11]

And it's hard to discount the importance of visuals. People like to enjoy what they're looking at while they drink, which plays a role in everything from the Champagne flute to elaborate tiki mugs and to the otherwise inexplicable popularity of blue curaçao.

5. Sip

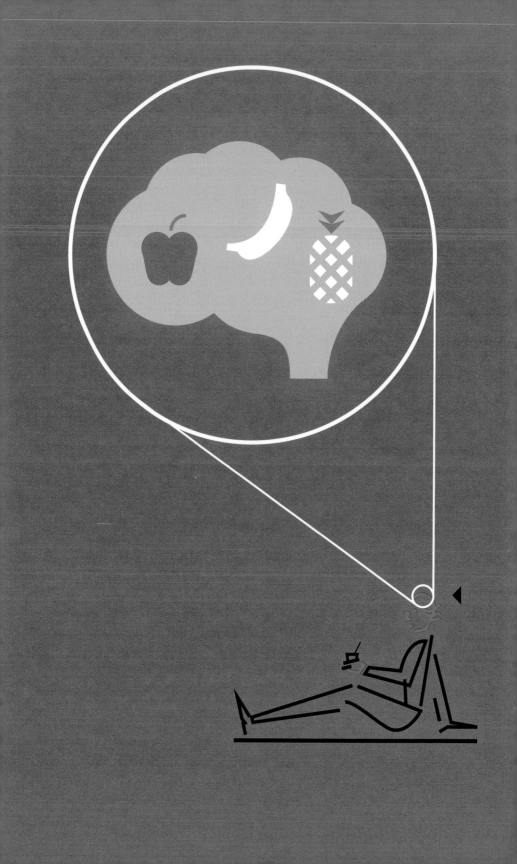

Tasting a drink may seem like the simplest thing in the world. After all, we taste things all the time—how complicated could something be if we do it every day without thinking?

If you take one thing away from this part of the book, let it be that the answer to that question is almost always *very*.

A lot goes into a sip. Flavor incorporates both the taste sensors on your tongue and the olfactory sensors in your nose in a dynamic and evolving way that's frustratingly difficult to study. The texture of the liquid, its temperature, an assortment of chemical reactions taking place inside your mouth, and the dozens of associations you have with different flavors all affect your perception of what you're drinking. Even experienced tasters have difficulty disentangling the knot.

Still think a sip is a simple proposition? Buckle up—it's about to get crazy in here.

How We Taste

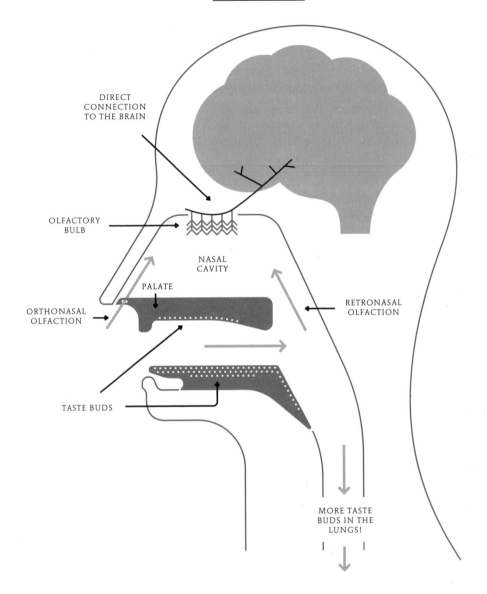

DIRECT
CONNECTION
TO THE BRAIN

OLFACTORY
BULB

NASAL
CAVITY

PALATE

ORTHONASAL
OLFACTION

RETRONASAL
OLFACTION

TASTE BUDS

MORE TASTE
BUDS IN THE
LUNGS!

Flavor is a combination of what we think of as taste and smell, although both are far more complicated than they appear. There are taste buds in many more places than just the surface of the tongue, and they're not arranged in a convenient map like you learned in grade school.

There are two different ways for smells to reach your nasal cavity (although your brain files stimuli from the back-of-the-throat route under "taste"), and signals from your olfactory receptors shoot directly into the parts of your brain involved in emotion and memory. All of this plays into the experience of everything you eat or drink.

Taste, Smell, and the Evolution of a Sip

Let's start with some basics. Your tongue is covered with little domes and protrusions (*papillae* is the technical term) that contain your taste buds. There are more of them in other places—the roof of your mouth, your esophagus, and even your lungs—but let's focus on the tongue for now.

In grade school you were probably taught that there are four or five basic tastes (the number depends on your teacher and how old you are), and that they map to certain areas of the tongue. Your teachers were wrong.

For one thing, taste receptors occur beyond the tongue, as noted above. For another, only certain taste receptors are unequally distributed—the ones in your lungs, for instance, exclusively sense bitterness. Each of the basic tastes can be detected all across your tongue.

Believe it or not, exactly what the basic tastes are is a subject of debate. Today virtually everyone accepts a minimum of five: sweet, salty, sour, bitter, and savory, although for a very long time science accepted only the first four. Some people argue that other things should be included, like fattiness or the burning and cooling sensations we feel when we consume things like hot peppers and mint.[1]

In any case, we're talking about only a handful of tastes. The major ones deal with energy intake (sweet), electrolytic balance (salty), avoiding poison (bitter), and so forth. They're like the foundation of a building: absolutely essential and probably not the thing of which the architect is most proud.

Let's be generous and assume we're underrating the tongue. Maybe there are ten basic tastes, or even twenty. Heck, make it a hundred. It doesn't matter. The number of tastes the tongue distinguishes will always be dwarfed by the vast universe of smells the nose can pick up.

How vast? Eighty million is the lowball estimate; in some cases, the figure could be over a trillion.

Y

"Hot" and "Cool" Pseudo-Flavors, p. 105

To be fair to the tongue, those millions of smells include both individual flavor chemicals like vanillin and limonene and various combinations of those and other chemicals. If we included combinations of tastes, the tongue would post better numbers too (albeit nothing in the trillions).

But it's also true that combinations of odor chemicals are encoded as distinct smells, in a way that combinations of tastes are not. If you drink vinegar with salt and MSG it'll taste sour, salty, and savory (and terrible). But a whiff of nutmeg doesn't smell like pine and citrus and camphor, even though all of those scents are in there—it just smells like nutmeg.

This vast array of odors is one reason bartenders will sometimes smell drinks as they're making them. You can get a very strong sense of how a thing will taste when you know how it fits into those eighty million scent combinations.

But smell alone is still not the full picture. Even if we set the tongue's contributions aside (which we should not do), the brain processes aromas differently depending on their source.

Orthonasal olfaction, which is what you're experiencing when something comes up through your nostrils, sends signals to your brain that get marked "nose." Retronasal olfaction, in which the smells waft up through your throat into the back of your nasal cavity, sends signals that get tagged "mouth." This is probably why you haven't thought about tasting as smelling before—your brain has been telling you they're separate.

Your throat's ability to "smell" is part of the reason the finish is a distinct part of the sip. When that drink hits the back of your throat it's got clearer access to your nasal cavity, and you'll get a big burst of volatile aromatics on the swallow. You'll also get new sensory input from the taste buds in your pharynx and esophagus as your drink is going down. So don't spit out your wine at a tasting—you'll miss out on a lot. If you take away anything from this section, let it be that.

Texture and Mouthfeel

Mouthfeel is a funny term. It describes a complicated set of only partially related phenomena, which makes it easy to forget that the definition is right there in the word. When you take a sip, what does your drink *feel* like?

One of the major factors to contribute to mouthfeel is viscosity, or how thick the liquid is. Depending on context, we might prefer a thicker or a thinner drink. If your English stout is thin and watery, for instance, you probably won't enjoy it much, while an American lager that feels heavy and thick is a terrible thing to bring to a barbecue.[2]

In general, dissolved solids will make your drink feel thicker, as will things like oils and proteins. The differences can be subtle, but the mouth is a very sensitive instrument. The sweeteners used in diet sodas produce a less viscous mixture than the ones used in regular sodas, and the difference in mouthfeel is perceptible.

Another component of mouthfeel is astringency, which shows up in "dry" beverages like gins and certain wines. Astringency creates the feeling that all the saliva has been sucked out of your mouth (thus, the descriptor *dry*). That qualitative description has some basis in science.

Chemically, an astringent is something that can bind to proteins and strip them out of whatever solution they're in. Ethanol, acetone, and tannins are known to have this power. Saliva contains lubricating proteins; strip them out, and your mouth will feel quite different and a lot drier.[3]

Mouthfeel is also affected by other things. Suspended solids (that is, solids that haven't dissolved) can give the liquid a grainy texture, which is usually unpleasant. Bubbles of carbon dioxide gas are often enjoyed for the tickling sensation they cause—though, surprisingly, the effect appears to depend more on the prickly and slightly painful presence of carbonic acid than on direct tactile stimulation by the bubbles. Carbonated beverages

Mouthfeel Wheel

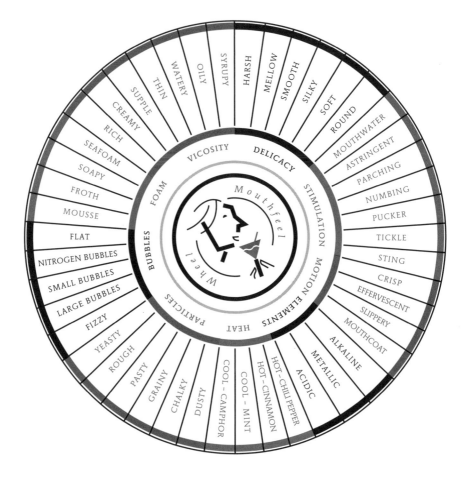

Flavor wheels are by their nature more evocative than precise, and mouthfeel wheels are even more so.

This one is meant to summarize mouthfeel characteristics across a variety of types of alcohol. Not every segment applies equally to every drink—"frothy" wines aren't especially common, for example—but there should be a few words here to describe whatever you're drinking.

consumed at pressures high enough to prevent bubbles from forming were still reported as having their signature bite. Still, it appears that bubbles enhance the effects of the acid.[4]

Visual Pre-Tasting

Some flavors and colors are very strongly associated with one another. You may have heard something described as tasting "red" or "purple," meaning that it has the same artificial cherry or grape flavor found in lollipops of those colors. The color is just convenient shorthand for a flavor we don't have a better name for. ("Artificial cherry" is a lot clunkier than "red," and the two descriptions mean the same thing in practice.) Names aside, taste expectations based solely on color can actually affect the way we perceive food and drinks.

A landmark study that you may find either hilarious or depressing, depending on your perspective, revealed that a group of oenology students couldn't tell white wine from red when food coloring was added.[5]

The research team, based at the University of Bordeaux—a place with a fairly good oenological reputation—asked a group of students to taste a red wine and a white one, and then to assess which wine was a better fit for a series of common flavor descriptors. The students matched the white wine to pear, honey, and other common white wine descriptors, while the red was matched to its common associations, such as pepper and black currant.

A week later the researchers brought back the same group of students and had them try two more wines under the same formula. The difference was that this time both samples were the same white wine: one had been dyed red with a flavor-neutral colorant, and the students were given every reason to believe that it was a normal red Bordeaux. Remarkably, they described the colored white wine using the red wine terms.

Wine Descriptors

		WHITE BORDEAUX WITH COLORING	UNCOLORED WHITE BORDEAUX
WHITE WINE	Lychee		••• • •
	Floral	••	• • • •• • • • ••• •• •
	Honey	•	• • • ••• • •
	Citrus	• •	•• • • •
	Passion fruit	•	• • • •••
	Apple	• •	• • • • • • •
	Banana	•	• • • •
	Candy	•	• • • •
	Pear	•	• • • ••
	Pineapple		• • •• ••
	Grapefruit	•	• • • • •
	Acacia		• •
	Peach	• •	• • • • • • •
	Butter	•	• •
RED WINE	Spice	• • •• •••••• •• • • • • •• •	• •
	Wooded	• • • • • • •	• •
	Blackcurrant	• • • •• • • •	• •
	Raspberry	•• • •• • •• • •	
	Cherry	• • • • • • •	
	Prune	• • • • • •	•
	Strawberry	• • • • • •	•
	Vanilla	• •	• • •
	Cinnamon	•	
	Pepper	••• • •• • •• ••• • • ••	• • • •
	Animal	• •••	•
	Licorice	• • •	

Given a list of common wine descriptors and asked to assign them to the two wines, oenology students overwhelmingly gave the ones associated with white wines to the wine that looked white, and the ones associated with red wines to the wine that looked red, even though they were exactly the same. Each of the descriptors in the table was used by at least three of the fifty-four subjects comparing uncolored white Bordeaux against the same wine with red food coloring added.

So was all that stuff about the power of smell pure nonsense? I wouldn't go that far—but it's pretty clear that it can be overridden sometimes.

A look at crème de violette may be instructive here. It's a floral, almost perfumy liqueur made from violet petals. It's also very purple, and some people who try crème de violette will taste cloying artificial grape, because the association with the color is so strong. A second sip with their eyes closed, however, will change this perception.[6]

Psychology of Taste

Let's paint a little picture. You're young. (But not too young. Don't drink under age, friends.) You've got a bottle of whatever you can get your hands on—it's bourbon, you think, but you don't really know what that means yet. It's a hot summer evening, and you and your sweetheart have gone down to the lake to watch the sun go down. You could not be more in love.

And that's where your memory takes you when you drink that same cheap bourbon from your youth.

Why is it that we form these kinds of strong associations with certain sensory experiences? That a whiff of the wrong perfume can make us miserable, or a sip of the right kind of rotgut can be sublime? It's all in the nose.

The olfactory bulb is unique among the sensory organs, in that it has direct connections to the amygdala and the hippocampus—regions of the brain involved in emotion and memory.[7] Given that our sense of smell exists, in part, to tell us what's food and what's poison, it makes sound evolutionary sense that it would be plugged right into our visceral response system in a way that our other senses aren't.

That this connection makes smell the most evocative sense is a beautiful by-product of evolution. Tasting, being heavily olfactory to begin with, gets the benefits of this effect.[8]

Y

Taste, Smell, and the Evolution of a Sip, p. 95

More Psychology, or
Does Expensive Booze Taste Better?

Yes, expensive booze does taste better—but not for the reasons you might think.

Wine has been the subject of a great deal of scientific research. One subject that has attracted a lot of interest is how well the price of wine correlates with its drinker's enjoyment. And the results are really not good news for the producers of expensive wines: as far as science is aware, if the average person likes a high-end wine more than an inexpensive one, it's probably because he or she knows how much the bottle cost.

A Caltech-Stanford team compared subjects' responses to two wines; participants were told that one sample was a five-dollar wine and that the other was a forty-five-dollar one. In fact, they were both the same wine. Perhaps predictably, the allegedly more expensive wine was ranked higher across the board.[9]

The kicker? The subjects were scanned using fMRI during the experiment, and they actually had more activity in an area of the brain associated with experiencing pleasantness while drinking the "more expensive" wine. This experiment wasn't a case of people just giving the "correct" answer after the fact—they actually liked the wine more on a chemical level.

On the other side of the experimental coin are comparisons between wines that have an actual difference in price. These results don't look any better for the winemakers. A major study from 2008 found that in blind tastings most people tend to like wines slightly *less* as they get more expensive. Wine experts who took part were an exception—their enjoyment went up. According to the study's authors, this distinction could reflect either an innate difference in taste processing that leads certain people to become oenologists, or the acquisition of particular tastes in the course of training and experience.[10]

Either case, though, means that the value of a wine expert's advice is extremely dependent on context. If you have some training and expertise, it may be very helpful. If not, there's a decent

chance you don't experience wine in the same way as a professional. Better to just get the most expensive bottle you can afford,
since just knowing its cost will prompt you to enjoy it.

Evolution of Tastes over a Lifetime

Nobody ever said getting old was easy, and I'm afraid I'm not
going to buck that trend. We all know that as people age they are
likely to experience a decline in their hearing and vision; by the
same token their senses of smell and taste begin to wane, too.

Your body is made of cells—gazillions of them. They're the basic
unit of life. Any individual cell has a much shorter life span than
you do, so your body is constantly making new ones to replace
the ones that die.

Many of the difficulties that come with age can be blamed on
malfunctions of this cell replacement system. As you get older
the sensory cells in your taste buds and olfactory bulb get worse
at replacing themselves, and you need more of whatever you're
tasting to get the effect you're used to. This is perhaps the kernel of truth in the stereotypical association between hard candies and the elderly. Hard candies are concentrated sugar, after
all—you'd need to lose a lot of taste buds before you couldn't taste
them anymore.

And speaking of candy fans, let's talk about kids for a moment.
You may have noticed that sweets tasted way, way better when you
were young than they do now. The sweet stuff hasn't changed—
you have. Children have a substantially greater preference for
sugar than adults do. There's an evolutionary logic here: kids
are still growing, and their systems need the raw energy simple
sugars provide. It's also probably true that the average adult has
spent more time getting acclimated to bitter flavors (coffee, broc-
coli, IPAs) than the average kid has.

But the craziest thing that feeds into those childhood sugar
cravings is that if you're young enough, and already have a sweet

tooth, just having sugar in your mouth can induce an analgesic reaction.

It's worth noting that "young enough" here is up to about age ten. Beyond that age, kids who receive more sugar than they care for don't feel the same pain-relieving effect. It's still pretty important news if you're ever going to be taking care of children. "Sugar high" isn't a misnomer—the stuff is literally a painkiller!

Effects of Temperature on Perception

We serve tea hot and cocktails cold (generally speaking). How did we come to the conclusion that these are the "right" temperatures? Some of our temperature preferences certainly came about by virtue of historical accident, but many are just tradition. The apple brandy Calvados is traditionally served scalding hot in Normandy, while freeze-distilled American applejack is generally served cold. Tea and coffee, though usually served hot, have very popular iced forms. And if the literally set-on-fire Blue Blazer isn't a cocktail, then I'm a Monkey Gland's uncle.

Still, those expectations about temperature have consequences. People tend to be very conservative about their food and drink (when was the last time you changed your cola brand?) and this applies to temperature as well. We pretty consistently like our drinks at the temperatures we're used to, irrespective of what they are.

But the reasons are not all psychological. A protein called TRPM5 (which is short for a much longer phrase than you might expect) shows up in high numbers on the tongue and is involved in tasting sweet, savory, and bitter flavors. This protein is very perceptibly stimulated by heat, which is convenient, because so is an increase in perceived sweetness.

Too straightforward for you? Don't worry—there's always a crazier fish. This time it's the phenomenon of thermal tasting, which is an innocuous-sounding term that literally means tasting temperature.

According to a Yale study from the tail end of the last millennium, about two-thirds of people have taste buds that can be stimulated by temperature changes alone. Sourness is perceived at about twenty-seven degrees below the normal temperature of the mouth; saltiness comes into play after a drop of forty-five.[11]

You can test this one on yourself very easily. Set an ice cube on the tip of your tongue and wait. As it gets colder, you may notice a sour or salty taste; once you remove the cube and let your tongue warm up again, you may notice a sweeter taste instead. If you do, congratulations: you're a thermal taster!

"Hot" and "Cool" Pseudo-Flavors

Way back in a previous section when I named the five basic tastes,[T] I can virtually guarantee that at least one of you was confused by the exclusion of "spicy." It's so clearly a thing! There are entire restaurants dedicated to it! This section, dear reader, is for you.

Taste, Smell, and the Evolution of a Sip, p. 95

Spiciness is a very real phenomenon, but it isn't a taste per se. It's a chemical trick played on your body.

The "hot" ingredients in chili peppers are capsaicin and its related compounds, known as capsaicinoids. Strangely enough, capsaicinoids are structurally related to the signature compounds of vanilla and cloves. The same goes for ginger, but that's not surprising—ginger has its own kind of heat.

Plants produce capsaicinoids for the same reason they make many aromatic chemicals—to discourage certain animals from eating them. You can tell from the success of Frank's RedHot cayenne pepper sauce that the plants failed in this endeavor spectacularly, but in principle capsaicinoids make the eating experience unpleasant by stimulating pain receptors in the mouth. Yes, that means eating spicy food is at least a little masochistic—but be honest, you knew that already.

Capsaicinoids also stimulate warmth receptors, and the brain does some simple math with that information: hot + painful =

burning. The body responds the same way it would to an actual source of heat, causing you to sweat and dilating your blood vessels to cool you down (which may also cause you to look flushed). The symptoms are more dramatic if the spicy food contacts particularly sensitive tissue, like the eyes; there's a reason this stuff is used in pepper spray.

It's also pretty well documented that capsaicin can trigger a pleasure response or even a high. One theory is that the body releases endorphins to mitigate the pain from a burn—and since you're not actually burning, you come out ahead. Another hypothesis is that the capsaicin pain overwhelms any other unpleasant sensations, making it a kind of backdoor painkiller. Regardless, people seem to enjoy spice for reasons beyond the flavor and a love of pain.

Capsaicin's super-powered opposite (which of them is the evil twin I'll leave to you) is menthol, a signature element of mint and a frequent cigarette additive. Where capsaicin activates your body's warmth sensors, menthol tickles the cells that register a cooling sensation. It's also a pain reliever—applied to burns, among other uses.

What's most remarkable is how well the powers of capsaicin and menthol are arranged against each other. The presence of menthol reduces capsaicin's effects if the two are taken simultaneously or the menthol leads by just a few minutes; but if there's a fifteen-minute lag time before the capsaicin is applied, the menthol actually makes the capsaicin's effect worse.

They make a fascinating pair, don't they? Just as temperature can induce or influence taste, ^Y these two flavor chemicals can convince your body that its temperature is rapidly changing. How anything gets done amid all this trickery is quite beyond me.

Y
*Effects of
Temperature
on
Perception,
p. 104*

Metabolism of Alcohol

To those of you who read the table of contents and skipped right to this section: greetings! And welcome to *Distilled Knowledge*. I promise you'll enjoy the earlier parts of this book when you get around to them.

It certainly seems that the most common questions I am asked are either forms of "How do I get drunker faster?" or variations on "How do I stay soberer longerer?" Well, friends, whichever is your goal, you will find the answers here. Please use them responsibly.

I highly recommend you read the sections on ethanol digestion and metabolism in the Appendix before you continue.[†] These processes will come into play throughout this chapter. But, if you'd like to get right down to business, here's what you need to know.

A drink of liquor passes through your mouth, down your esophagus, and into your stomach, where it stays for some period of time. Although a portion of the alcohol is absorbed

Y
Ethanol Digestion, p. 172, *Ethanol Metabolism,* p. 174

How Alcohol Is Absorbed

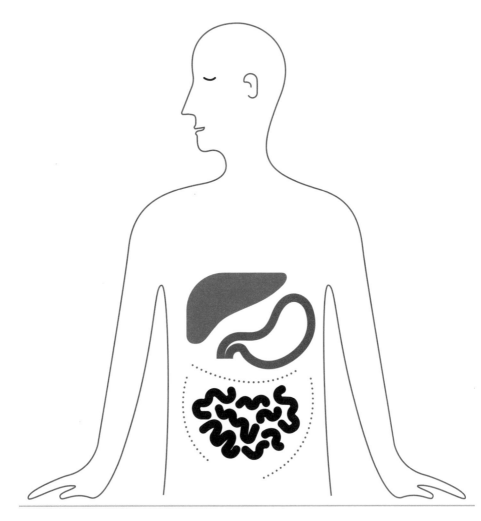

STOMACH

The stomach is involved in both absorption and metabolism. Between 10 and 30 percent of the ethanol that makes it into your blood will be absorbed in the stomach, depending on how full it is; but your drink will also be exposed to alcohol dehydrogenase, breaking down some of the ethanol before it can be absorbed.

SMALL INTESTINE

The vast majority of alcohol absorption takes place here—between 70 and 90 percent. The small intestine has thin walls with a high surface area and densely packed blood vessels, perfect conditions for the booze to seep into your blood.

LIVER

Blood leaving the stomach and intestines stops at the liver before it goes into general circulation. The liver is a filter for toxins, and it's where the bulk of alcohol metabolism takes place; but ethanol elimination is a slow process, and the liver can't keep up once your BAC gets above about .02.

into the blood there, most of the absorption happens in the small intestine.

Once in the blood, your drink's first stop is the liver. The liver produces an enzyme called alcohol dehydrogenase (also found in the stomach, in smaller quantities), which is the primary agent by which ethanol is metabolized.

Simple enough, right? Now, without further ado, I invite you to enjoy this handy guide to what's good and bad for your buzz.

Drink Strength

"This seems obvious enough," you may be thinking. "Surely stiffer drinks lay you out faster."

Surprisingly, no. Or, at least, not exactly.

The aspect of digestion you'll need to know is that the stomach regulates how much stuff it lets through to the small intestine, and it does so in part based on what it contains. If there's a lot of digestive work to be done, the stomach hangs onto its contents longer; if there isn't, it doesn't. For a thorough discussion of this process, see the Appendix.

Y
Ethanol Digestion, p. 172

Liquor before Beer, You're in the Clear

Strangely enough, this saying may have some truth to it (emphasis on *may*).

We know that spirits above a certain strength are actually more poorly absorbed into the bloodstream, because they prompt the stomach to seal up and spend more time digesting the booze. It's conceivable that whatever you drink after that first shot will be subject to the same effects, if there's still some hard liquor in your stomach keeping it on lockdown.

Have I seen any direct evidence that this is true? Nope. But it's consistent with other things that definitely are, so who knows?

It might make intuitive sense that a large meal—or any quantity of big and complex molecules—would create more work for the stomach and thereby slow down the process of digestion. Curiously enough, a strong drink does the same thing.

As you surely know, above a certain dose alcohol can do very unpleasant things to you. Your body doesn't want those things to happen to you. So when it notices a shot of overproof whiskey hitting the floor of your stomach, it sends the signal to seal up: the pyloric sphincter, which is the gateway between your stomach and your intestines, closes off, and the liquor is trapped in the stomach for a longer period of time.

As I've said, some of the alcohol is absorbed into your blood through the stomach walls, but a majority of the absorption takes place in your intestines, which are much more efficient at this sort of thing. On an empty stomach, about 10 percent of the total absorbed ethanol takes the stomach-wall route.

While it's in the stomach, the ethanol in that shot is exposed to alcohol dehydrogenase—the same enzyme that the liver produces to process it out of your system.[T] By the time that drink gets to your small intestine, there's actually less of it left to be absorbed.

Peak ethanol absorption happens when your drink is around 20 to 25 percent alcohol by volume. That's about the percentage you'll find in a lot of cocktails or a fifty-fifty highball (that is, hard liquor and soda). As drinks get stronger than that, the body's reaction to them gets disproportionately stronger; as they get weaker, there's simply less ethanol for the body to take in.

Y
*Ethanol
Metabolism,
p. 174*

Drinking Speed

"Let me guess," you're probably thinking. "Now you're going to tell us drinking faster keeps you sober, right?"

Fortunately, no. There is still some sense in the world. How quickly you drink is one of the most important factors in how much of a buzz you get. It seems obvious that this would be so—

add more, have more—but the mechanism is quite interesting. It has to do with the enzyme that does the bulk of the work in processing the booze out of your system.[T]

It doesn't take much ethanol to overwhelm the amount of alcohol dehydrogenase in your liver—a blood alcohol concentration (BAC) of about .02 is enough to do the job. In other words, your body has a cap on how much alcohol it's able to metabolize and eliminate per hour, whether your BAC is at .02, .08, or .40. Once you cross the .02 threshold you're getting drunk faster than your body can sober you up.

It may help to compare this process to a bucket with a leak in the bottom. Sure, there's water dripping out all the time, but if you add more water fast enough, the level in the bucket will still rise, because only so much water can leave at once. Ethanol in your blood follows the same pattern.

This may not seem to square with what we learned in the last section.[TT] If getting a lot of ethanol into your system very quickly gets you drunker, shouldn't that mean a shot of hard liquor will affect you more than a beer? It might, and it often will, but we can't predict a general rule from what we have so far. Strength

Ethanol Metabolism, p. 174

Drink Strength, p. 111

Beer before Liquor, Never Been Sicker

If there's a grain of truth to this saying, it probably has to do with drinking speed. Consider a beer and a shot, each containing the same total amount of ethanol: if you were to drink them at the same rate, you'd finish the shot a lot faster. It's possible that we get used to a certain drinking speed over the course of an evening, and when we suddenly switch to something much stronger we fail to adjust our consumption rate, ultimately drinking more and getting ill.

This is possible, but not certain or universal. It's worth being wary if you've run afoul of this proverb in the past, but if you've never worried about it before, you have no reason to start now.

and speed are independent variables. For instance, if you knocked back a 40 percent ABV (alcohol by volume) shot of applejack in one gulp, it would hit you harder than the same drink sipped over a longer period of time. Ditto for a 20 percent ABV Orange Blossom. Trying to guess whether the shot or the sipped cocktail will build up a bigger buzz would be (very much) like comparing apples and oranges.

Water Intake

Given that higher ethanol concentrations tend to lead to lower BACs (above 25 percent, anyhow), does that mean that having water while drinking is a bad idea? At least if you want to stay sober?

No, it's definitely still a good idea. For starters, drinking tends to dehydrate you,[Y] and it's likely you're already not drinking enough water. Make your life easier in the morning by having some now.

But how well hydrated you are also affects how drunk you can get. Ethanol rapidly disperses throughout all the water in your body. The less water there is, the higher the concentration of ethanol you'll reach while consuming a given number of drinks.[YY]

Drinking water also helps by slowing down your consumption. It takes more time to drink five cocktails if you have a glass of water after each one, and that gives your liver more time to catch up.[YYY]

It also gives you a chance to notice that you're in a good place, before you have the drink that could take you to a bad one.

Y
Dehydration,
p. 143

YY
Muscle,
Weight, and
Body Water,
p. 123

YYY
Drinking
Speed,
p. 112

Food Intake

Possibly the oldest advice on how to stay sober is to drink on a full stomach. The usual stated reason for this is that the food absorbs the alcohol. While I can't say for sure that it doesn't, keep in mind that your body is trying to break down and absorb that food, too. Whatever ethanol gets soaked into the food may still find its way into your blood.

But food also affects the rate of gastric emptying.[T] When you eat a big meal, the sphincter that separates your stomach from your intestines closes off (after all, your stomach can't do its digestive job if big chunks of food can slip right out of it). So if you drink with or after a meal, your glass of wine is stuck in the stomach, where it gets exposed to alcohol dehydrogenase and broken down. It can't just sneak through to the intestines to be absorbed, nor can the ethanol just be sucked into starchy bread and quietly smuggled out of your body.

Ethanol Digestion, p. 172

On a full stomach, about 30 percent of the total ethanol you've taken in will be absorbed through the gastric walls, which is a higher percentage than would be absorbed by an empty stomach. But you can also expect your peak BAC to be about 60 percent lower than it would be if you drank on an empty stomach. One study found that the effect of stiffer drinks leading to a lower BAC[TT] is even stronger on a full stomach; 4 percent ABV solutions led to drunker subjects than 16 and 40 percent ones.[1]

Drink Strength, p. 111

Eating also appears to speed up ethanol metabolism, according to a Swedish study that tested subjects who were fed five hours after drinking. Alcohol was removed from their blood at rates ranging from 36 to 50 percent faster than usual. In other words, not only can eating help you avoid getting drunk, it can even help you sober up long after the fact. No wonder we love greasy late-night food so much.[2]

Food Types

Advice on how to stay sober often goes further than the simple directive "drink with food" to include recommendations on particular things to eat. This is normally an injunction to stick to carbohydrates, proteins, or fats, depending on who's giving the advice. A study designed to tease out the differences among these three macronutrients found reductions in peak BAC to be similar across all of them, on the order of 50 percent, with protein making the strongest showing.[3]

If one of our standard assumptions is that more time in the stomach means less ethanol can be absorbed into the bloodstream, it makes sense that things the stomach needs to spend more time breaking down should slow the gastric emptying process—and consequently help maintain sobriety. Big, complicated molecules fit that bill. Experiments have even confirmed that longer fatty acid salts slow down gastric emptying more than shorter ones do.[4]

Ethanol Digestion, p. 172, Drink Strength, p. 111

The thing is, protein, fat, and carbohydrate are all big categories, and the molecules they refer to range widely in size and complexity. Rather than worry about which type of food you're eating, focus on how much food you consume; the difference in BAC reduction between the best and worst performers was much, much smaller than the difference between the worst and nothing. More food is better than less food, and some food is better than no food. And if you want to be especially careful, go for the chicken before the bread and butter.

Food Intake, p. 114

There is, however, one nutrient you can consume that will definitely help you stay sober: fructose. If you've taken organic chemistry, you already know that if a molecule ends in *-ose* it's a carbohydrate, and the simplest carbohydrates are the sugars. Sucrose is common table sugar, lactose is the one that makes milk taste slightly sweet, and fructose is a sugar found in fruits, some vegetables, and high-fructose corn syrup.

Fructose will reduce your peak blood alcohol concentration by about 14 percent, according to one study. The subjects were given dinner, followed by about two shots' worth of whiskey (being a medical test subject sounds nice, doesn't it?) with an equal amount of water, and then either plain water or water with sixty grams (about two ounces) of fructose dissolved in it. Most of the subjects who got the fructose had a lower peak BAC, and all of them had lower total ethanol absorption.[5]

Blood Alcohol Concentration V. Other Factors

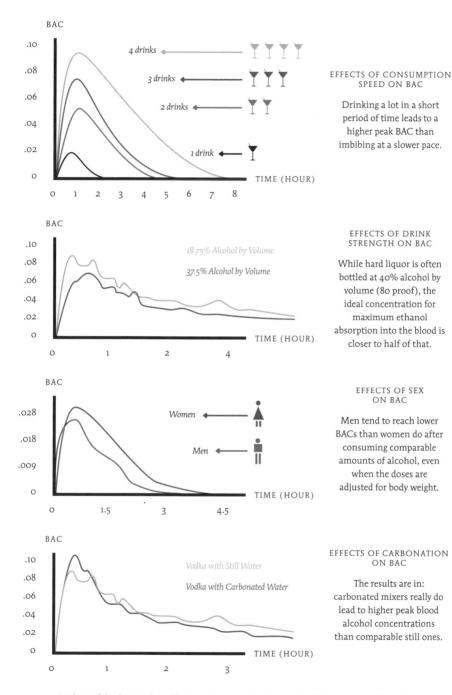

EFFECTS OF CONSUMPTION SPEED ON BAC

Drinking a lot in a short period of time leads to a higher peak BAC than imbibing at a slower pace.

EFFECTS OF DRINK STRENGTH ON BAC

While hard liquor is often bottled at 40% alcohol by volume (80 proof), the ideal concentration for maximum ethanol absorption into the blood is closer to half of that.

EFFECTS OF SEX ON BAC

Men tend to reach lower BACs than women do after consuming comparable amounts of alcohol, even when the doses are adjusted for body weight.

EFFECTS OF CARBONATION ON BAC

The results are in: carbonated mixers really do lead to higher peak blood alcohol concentrations than comparable still ones.

A subset of the factors that affect intoxication. Note that each of these graphs reflects the results of a particular experiment: the numbers may not hold for every drinking situation, but the general patterns should.

Why on earth would this be so? Fructose appears to help the liver make new alcohol-processing enzymes from used ones, effectively raising the cap on how much you can drink without overwhelming your liver.[6]

Note that we're talking only about pure fructose, here. Don't start adding synthetic grenadine to your drinks just because it contains high-fructose corn syrup; there haven't been studies on the effects of the other chemicals it contains, separately or in combination with fructose. Even fresh fruits aren't necessarily safe.[7]

Ⴈ
Grapefruit's Effects, p. 120

Carbonation's Effects

"I should have stuck to wine," thought the wedding guest the morning after. "Why, oh, why did I have to drink the *Champagne?*"

Long the signature drink of celebration, Champagne has acquired a reputation for aiding and abetting intoxication. All beverages with bubbles have this reputation, to varying degrees. There are even stories out there about veteran whiskey drinkers getting knocked flat by a few beers.

Believe it or not, this one's true. A study from the University of Manchester (that's England, not New Hampshire) compared peak blood alcohol concentrations after participants drank vodka in three ways: straight, with water, and with carbonated water. The bubbles gave the biggest buzz.

If you've ever burped, you know that gas can accumulate in the stomach. (If you've never burped, see a doctor.) Sodas and fermented goods contain dissolved carbon dioxide gas, which builds up in your gut.

Two mechanisms have been proposed to explain how that translates into a higher BAC. It's possible that the added pressure speeds up gastric emptying, so the ethanol spends less time getting preprocessed in the stomach. It has also been suggested that the added pressure increases absorption through the stomach lining. It may even be that both are true.

But if you're just worried about the effect and not the reason: yes, Champagne will hit you harder than wine of equal proof, and beverages made with a home carbonation system pack the biggest punch of all.

Drink Temperature

It is widely claimed that hot drinks result in greater ethanol absorption, and the most common explanation for this assertion holds that it is due to easier absorption into the bloodstream by wide-open blood vessels in the mouth.

No study seems to have been done on this topic explicitly, but there are a few on related topics that seem to suggest it's possible.

First, it has been suggested that applying heat to an area results in increased blood flow, more permeable blood vessels, or some kind of black magic (the precise mechanism has not been confirmed) resulting in easier absorption of substances across any local membranes. For example, a study on nicotine patches showed that heating the area of application led, on average, to blood nicotine levels thirteen times higher than expected after thirty minutes. That's a lot. It's something like getting half a pack's worth of nicotine in one cigarette.[7]

The authors of the study point out that further research is needed to confirm that this isn't a nicotine-specific effect. That's fair, but they were also able to demonstrate increased blood flow to the affected region. And let's not forget that the membranes in the digestive system are *supposed* to have things getting absorbed across them, while your body really never intended your skin to serve that purpose.

It is therefore reasonable to imagine that the rate of absorption across, say, the membranes in your mouth could be elevated by heat. But thirteen times something very small would still be something small, and a drink still spends too little time in your mouth for these effects to matter much.

If there is truth to this claim, the heat probably makes a bigger difference in the stomach, where a small but nontrivial percentage of absorption takes place. There is also evidence that a hot meal empties out of the stomach faster than a cold one does, which lends extra plausibility to this one.[8]

So, what's the bottom line on your hot schnappsolate? It hasn't been proven to bring your evening to an early end, but it hasn't been disproven either. And there is some indirect evidence that it could.

Grapefruit's Effects

There are lots of rumors that grapefruit juice makes drinks more potent. For a start, it's known to increase the potency of certain prescription drugs. In fact, it's specifically contraindicated by a frighteningly long list of pharmaceuticals. (If you're on any kind of medication, it's not a bad idea to talk to your doctor before you drink the stuff.)

We know this because grapefruit juice was used to mask the taste of the liquor in a study on interactions between the blood-pressure drug felodipine and ethanol. Surprising precisely everyone, the felodipine-grapefruit interaction was much, much stronger than the one they were trying to test: those who got just the drug had only about a fifth as much of it in their systems as the ones drinking the Felodipine Greyhounds.[9]

This reaction happens because something in grapefruit juice inhibits an important digestive enzyme, cytochrome P450 3A4 (which bears the charming nickname CYP3A4). Found in the liver and the intestine, CYP3A4 does a substantial job of metabolizing many drugs before they reach the bloodstream—the majority of felodipine, for instance, is processed out in this way, except when grapefruit interferes.

So, what are the implications for ethanol? The grapefruit trick should work only if ethanol is metabolized by CYP3A4, which it is not known to be, or if it turns out that grapefruit also inhibits one of ethanol's normal metabolizing enzymes, which it is not known to do.[10] Maddeningly, that first felodipine study didn't track blood alcohol concentration—although, since it wasn't an intoxication study, it might not have had much to tell us if it had. So we can't confirm that the grapefruit-alcohol rumor isn't true, but the available evidence doesn't seem to support it. Unless grapefruit has a second mechanism that hasn't been discovered or ethanol is acted on by another enzyme that we don't know about, a Hemingway Daiquiri is no more dangerous than the standard variety.

Psychological Influences on Intoxication

Do you ever feel you get more of a buzz in certain places or when you're drinking with certain people? Or that you have to stay away from certain drinks, because they affect you disproportionately? You may be onto something—but probably not for the reasons you think.

Alcohol renders you subject to something called an expectancy effect. Part of your experience of drinking is what you anticipate it's going to be like: if you think you're going to get drunk, you probably will.

This theory was tested in what might be my favorite experiment in this book. Researchers in New Zealand set up a bar in their laboratory, complete with bartenders serving "Vodka Tonics," which were actually just tonic water poured out of a vodka bottle mixed with tonic water poured the regular way.

Half the participants were told they were getting plain tonic water. The other half were told they were getting vodka, too; their glasses were rimmed in vodka-soaked limes to smell like booze. After their drinks, they were all given a memory test.

The participants who thought they'd been drinking were both more suggestible and more confident in their final answers than the control group, just as drunk people would be. The women got giggly, and the men tried to hit on one of the researchers (come on, guys). They were all very surprised to learn that they'd been sober the whole time, because they *felt* drunk.[11]

Other studies have shown that people get more aggressive and more turned on when drinking what they're told is alcohol, even when it isn't.[12]

It makes some sense that a portion of the effects of drinking could be brought on psychologically. What, really, is the difference between *being* disinhibited and *acting* that way because you think you already are?

This could apply in all kinds of situations. Does the first sip hit you harder than any subsequent sip? It might be that you're flipping the subconscious "I'm drinking" switch, and so you start feeling the effects before they could possibly have started. Maybe you're dead sure that mixing hot grapefruit juice with your vodka will get you sloshed.[T] If you just believe hard enough, it probably will.

Ⴘ
*Drink
Temperature,
p. 119,
Grapefruit's
Effects,
p. 120*

Grape or Grain but Never the Twain

In general, claims that pairing different types of alcohol can affect a person in varying ways fall into one of two categories: The first is that they have no basis in truth; the second is that they're true in individual cases for idiosyncratic reasons. If you believe you'll get especially drunk by downing beer and wine in the same night, you just might, insofar as intoxication is a psychological phenomenon. If you have a strong memory of their commingled smells, viscerally associated with nausea, mixing them will probably make you sick.

But in all likelihood, you have nothing to worry about here besides taste—the flavors of beer and wine often mix poorly, which is a perfectly valid reason to stick to just one or the other on a given night.

Psychological Influences on Consumption

How good do you think you are at gauging your alcohol consumption? There's a decent chance you're worse at it than you think you are.

A British researcher found that beer served in glasses with different shapes was drunk at different speeds. People seem to judge how much they've had by how much they have left, which they're fine at estimating in cylindrical glasses but very poor at judging in tapered glasses (you know, the kind you normally drink beer out of at a bar).

What was the difference? Glasses with angled sides were emptied in seven minutes, versus eleven minutes for the cylinders. That's about a third less time. It may not seem like much, but when was the last time you said, "I'd like to go drinking for seven minutes"? Imagine it as three beers every twenty-two minutes versus two—or nine versus six in an hour. It adds up.[13]

Meanwhile, a French team found that loud music can increase the rate of consumption. Whether this is because it makes people more primed to drink, or because it makes it harder to talk and there's less else to do, they aren't sure. But in either case, the patrons in the study tended to order one more drink when the music was louder and to finish their drinks an average of three minutes faster.[14]

Muscle, Weight, and Body Water

Ever heard that heavier people tend to have a higher alcohol tolerance? Or that people with a lot of muscle can drink more than anyone else, because muscle is more efficient than other tissues at metabolizing alcohol?

Right on the results; wrong on the cause. Remember: the liver does the overwhelming majority of the work metabolizing your booze, the stomach comes in second, and the rest of the body's role is negligible. Sure, there are metabolic enzymes in muscle tissue (and everywhere else), but you'll get rid of more ethanol by exhaling it than by breaking it down in your biceps.

The reason the well muscled can drink more is that alcohol intoxication is, in part, a function of the body's total water content. Ethanol can be mixed with water in any proportion, and it spreads throughout the body by passive diffusion,[T] so it will get pretty much everywhere. Since our baseline for intoxication is the alcohol in the system as a percentage of the volume of the body's liquids (blood, serum, etc.), there are two ways to increase sobriety: lower the amount of ethanol or dilute it by increasing the amount of water.

Ethanol
Digestion,
p. 172

Every tissue in the body contains some water, even your bones. But muscles have more water than fat tissues do, which means that more muscular people are able to dilute the ethanol they consume more easily.

This is also the reason larger people generally have a higher tolerance for liquor: if two people have the same ratio of muscle to fat, the bigger one will have more total water because there's simply more of him or her.

Sex Differences in Metabolism

Let me be clear: there are no hard and fast rules about which of any two individuals is going to get drunk before the other. I know women who could drink a Russian sailor under the table. But individual variation can be quite broad without disproving a general trend, and in most cases a woman going drink for drink with a man will end up drunker than he will.

A study performed at the University of Trieste (Italy) found peak BAC to be about 20 percent higher for women than men given the same amount of ethanol (adjusted for body weight), which the researchers believe is due to reduced gastric metabolism of ethanol in women. The drinks were administered after a large breakfast, so the alcohol should have spent extra time in the stomach, exposed to gastric alcohol dehydrogenase.[TT]

Food Intake,
p. 114

The researchers measured alcohol dehydrogenase activity in the stomach and found it to be 40 percent lower in the women than it was in the men. Other studies have confirmed the theory that men produce more of this enzyme in the stomach than women do.

Put simply, both men and women get rid of some of the ethanol they consume before it reaches their blood, but men get rid of more at this earlier stage.[15]

Women also tend to have lower total body water than men do, which means it takes a smaller number of drinks to get to the same blood alcohol concentration.[T] On average, women are smaller than men and have more soft tissue and less muscle pound for pound. This means that if an average man and an average woman absorb the same amount of ethanol into their bloodstream, the woman will end up with a higher BAC.

Muscle, Weight, and Body Water, p. 123

On the other hand, women outperform men when it comes to alcohol elimination. That is, if a man and a woman have reached the same blood alcohol concentration and both stop drinking, the woman will reach complete sobriety first. The cause isn't fully understood, but one theory is that alcohol dehydrogenase activity in the liver is inhibited by dihydrotestosterone, a male reproductive hormone. So, fellas, if you find yourself staying drunk longer than your friends, feel free to tell them it just means you're more of a man.

Aging and Alcohol Consumption

Let's assume for a moment that you have aged in a healthy and graceful manner. You've managed to avoid liver disease, daily medications, and any major health complaints. I may have some good news for you.

Metabolism of ethanol was previously assumed to slow down with age, but studies show it actually does nothing of the kind, at least in the liver. The stomach is a different story, and guys may see their competitive advantage in gastric metabolism evaporate after age fifty. That's ultimately not that substantial of a loss, since the liver does most of the work.[16]

Total body water[T] does tend to decrease with age, but not by all that much and mostly as a result of the loss of muscle mass (or exchange of muscle for fat). Even better news is that recent studies have indicated that you don't have to lose muscle mass as you age—it's more likely a consequence of becoming more sedentary than it is of getting older.[17]

Stay healthy and active and you'll be able to get good and loaded at your seventy-fifth high school reunion.

Muscle, Weight, and Body Water, p. 123

The Little Flakes in Goldschläger

Debunking this rumor is nice and easy. If you haven't heard this story before, Goldschläger is a brand of cinnamon schnapps that's bottled with little flakes of gold in it. It's actually not the only spirit to get this treatment; a handful of distillers in Switzerland and Germany think their spirits deserve such a royal touch.

The gold flakes look pretty and add a certain decadence to the drinking experience. At some point, consumers began to believe that the little flakes also lacerated the throat on the way down, allowing the alcohol in the drink to bypass the stomach and liver and hit the system directly.

Is it true? Absolutely not.

Goldschläger uses twenty-four karat gold in its bottles. Or it claims to, at least, and there isn't a lot of reason to doubt the company. Twenty-four karat—that is, pure—gold is very, very soft. It's soft enough that it isn't recommended for use in everyday jewelry, never mind as a cutting edge.

Gold's particular variety of softness is malleability, which basically means the atoms in a sheet of gold move past one another very easily and is the reason gold can be made into those thin flakes in the first place. It's different from the flexibility of, say, paper, which bends very easily but can still cut you: at the molec-

Goldschläger

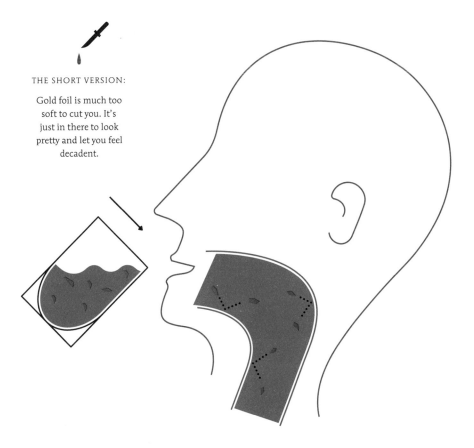

THE SHORT VERSION:

Gold foil is much too soft to cut you. It's just in there to look pretty and let you feel decadent.

ular level paper is fairly rigid. This is why we fold paper, and not gold, to make airplanes (OK, it's *one* reason).

Don't believe me? If you've got a bottle of Goldschläger handy, pour yourself a glass and pick out one of the little flakes. You should be able to twist, bend, and crumple it without too much effort. You should be completely unharmed in this process. If you do manage to cut yourself, sue Goldschläger and not me—it means they're not using twenty-four karat gold.

"But Brian," you say. "I definitely get good and toasted faster on Goldschläger. Surely there must be a reason?" Certainly: Goldschläger is 107 proof.

Yes, the silly schnapps with the little gold flakes packs more of a wallop than Jägermeister, tequila, many overproof whiskeys, and some absinthes. Lots of people don't realize that because it tastes like cinnamon candy, but if you dump a few shots into your hot chocolate, you'll be going nowhere fast.

7. Effects

Ah, intoxication—that most pleasant feeling. It makes speech flow more freely, translates desire into action, dulls the senses, elevates the heart rate, increases urination, and...wait, *what?*

We drink, at least in part, because we enjoy the euphoria of drunkenness, the effects on the mind that stimulate us and make us more sociable. But drinking is more complicated than that, because ethanol permeates *everything*. When you drink, that little fat- and water-soluble molecule will find its way into every nook and cranny of your body. It does a lot more than just make you warm and friendly.[1]

This chapter covers alcohol's effects on the body, including those during and beyond intoxication. It goes without saying that if you're experiencing any of the effects described in this chapter, you should not get behind the wheel of a car.

Symptoms of Intoxication

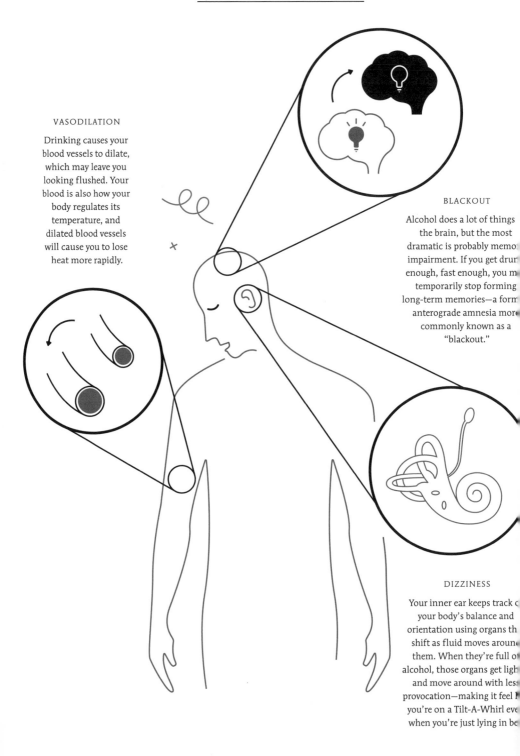

VASODILATION

Drinking causes your blood vessels to dilate, which may leave you looking flushed. Your blood is also how your body regulates its temperature, and dilated blood vessels will cause you to lose heat more rapidly.

BLACKOUT

Alcohol does a lot of things the brain, but the most dramatic is probably memo: impairment. If you get drur enough, fast enough, you m temporarily stop forming long-term memories—a form anterograde amnesia more commonly known as a "blackout."

DIZZINESS

Your inner ear keeps track your body's balance and orientation using organs th shift as fluid moves aroun them. When they're full of alcohol, those organs get ligh and move around with less provocation—making it feel you're on a Tilt-A-Whirl eve when you're just lying in be

Pleasure and Disinhibition

Let's start with the obvious: alcohol makes you feel good. This is a well-known fact across cultures and has been established for thousands of years. As is often the case, it took scientists a little while to confirm that something so obvious was true but confirm it they have.[2]

In 2012 a California team did a brain-imaging study on twenty-five people to obtain a visualization of the effects of alcohol immediately after consumption. They found that drinking triggered an endorphin release in all the subjects.[3]

Endorphins are your body's natural drugs. They do two things that are important, for our purposes: gunk up the pain-notification system and encourage the release of dopamine. The process of drinking stimulates the brain's reward centers, making us feel as if we're doing something good and inducing a desire to repeat the behavior.[4]

Can you think of anything else that reduces pain and encourages (at least some) people to go back for seconds? That's right: opiates. Drugs like morphine and heroin mimic the natural action of endorphins; they all bind to the same receptors, which we call "opioid receptors" because we figured out how they work with the artificial substances first. The point is, alcohol uses a natural, indirect pathway to trigger the same sensors that heavy-duty painkillers do. This may explain why opiate users also tend to have higher rates of alcoholism.

Another set of sensors that seems to be triggered by the pleasure chemicals that ethanol encourages your body to release is the cannabinoid receptors (bet you can't guess where *that* name comes from); they seem to be involved in drinking to excess, at least among rodent-Americans.

So, if you're wondering why ethanol feels good, there are two good reasons: it's a painkiller, with parallel action to two categories of very popular drugs; and it activates the reward pathway in your brain.

Now, if you're wondering why ethanol causes disinhibition, that's a whole different ball game. We normally think of alcohol as something that makes it harder for us to obey the rules of normal society—people have deep conversations, kiss strangers, and urinate on government buildings when they're drinking, because while sober they're constantly resisting the impulse to do these things. Essentially, alcohol messes with the brain in ways that lower your ability to control yourself. The adages "Drunk mind, sober heart" and *in vino veritas* describe this theory to a T.

But this idea is far from universally accepted in scientific circles, and even the word *disinhibition*, with all its connotations, is controversial. An alternative hypothesis is that alcohol puts us in an entirely different headspace, for psychological rather than physiological reasons. This is called the time-out theory, because it suggests that we mentally separate occasions when we drink from nondrinking situations and assume different rules for each. The time-out theory thus leaves the door open to suggestion, expectation, and habit as the determinants of behavior while we're drinking, which is extremely consistent with evidence that intoxication is a heavily psychological phenomenon.[Y]

Y
*Psychological
Influences on
Intoxication,
p. 121*

And think about it. If you're feeling pleasant and free of pain in an environment where the rules are different from normal life—which you're conditioned to expect will be freeing—won't you feel disinhibited? I bet you will. It's the same reason you can enjoy Burning Man without doing any drugs.

Imbalance and the Spins

A sad but true fact: if you get drunk enough, you'll get dizzy. The sensation may even last until the next morning, serving as a reminder that you should wait a little while before repeating your bad decisions. What causes it?

To begin with, the body regulates balance through a complicated matrix of sensory signals (*well* beyond the scope of this book). At every moment information from your eyes, muscles and joints, and inner ear is being compiled in your brain and turned into a picture of your orientation, speed, and acceleration—and it's done so well and so immediately that you don't even realize it. The body is an amazing piece of equipment sometimes.

The component of that whole complicated process that is most verifiably affected by drinking is the inner ear, a part of your body you've probably never thought about before. It's a weird organ—it handles both hearing and balance regulation—and it looks like an intergalactic snail.

The inner ear has three fluid-filled loops, called the semicircular canals, which are arranged on the body's three major axes of movement. If you tilt, nod, or turn your head, one of these canals will be disproportionately affected.

Anytime you move your head, those solid, attached canals move with you, but the fluid (called "endolymph") lags a bit because of its inertia. If you've tried to carry a very full glass and had the liquid slosh back toward you, you've encountered the same principle.

The canals contain sensory organs that move with respect to the fluid, much like the air bubble in a level. These sensors report their positions to the brain, which then determines whether the head is turning or shaking, based on this and other data.[5]

In order for the ear's positioning system to work, there needs to be a very precise and predictable relationship between the fluid and those sensory organs. For most people most of the time, this isn't a problem. But alcohol can change that relationship, and when it does, the brain doesn't know how to adjust.

There are two characteristics of alcohol that are particularly important here: it mixes easily with water, and it is also noticeably lighter than water. The sensory organs in the ear's semicircular canals are full of capillaries, which are full of blood, which is mostly water. When you're hammered, ethanol rapidly diffuses into that space in the capillaries.

Ethanol doesn't mix into the endolymph—that fluid we were talking about earlier—nearly as quickly. This means the sensory organs tend to move more easily relative to that fluid than they normally would—in other words, you don't have to move your head as much to make them slosh around.[6]

One of the things your body hates most is conflicting sensory information; if the ear says you're moving while everything else says you're standing still, it confuses the brain a lot. You know that feeling as dizziness, and possibly as motion sickness as well.

If the room *looks* like it's spinning, as well as feels like it, that's your brain overcompensating. When you move your head, your brain tells your eyes to move in the opposite direction so that you can keep looking at the same point. This is an important correction, because your head makes slight movements all the time that you probably don't even notice.

But in this situation there's nothing to correct for—you've simply had a few too many drinks and your body's signals have gotten scrambled. Your inner ear says you're spinning, and your brain tells your eyes to spin in the opposite direction to make up for it. It's impossible to focus on one spot, because your brain thinks your eyes need to move in order to do so. If you're this drunk you may feel as if you can't control your eyes—though you may be too distracted by the nausea to really notice.

There's good news, though: this disorientation is only temporary. Once you're done drinking and everything you've consumed has been absorbed into your blood, the ethanol content of the endolymph can start to catch up with the ethanol content of those sensory organs. When all of the liquids involved are equally lightened by the ethanol, your body's balance is restored, and the brain knows how to process the signals it's receiving again.

Well, temporarily, anyway. As the alcohol is processed out of your blood, those sensory organs return to their normal weight much faster than the endolymph does, which throws the brain's calculations off once again—but in the opposite direction. A funny consequence of this is that whichever way the room is spinning when you go to sleep, it might be spinning the other way when you wake up.

All this explains the old Dean Martin quip, "You're not drunk if you can lie on the floor without holding on." The good news is that Martin was wrong. You can have a nice buzz going without getting dizzy, so long as you're not flooding your inner ears with so much booze that they can't stay balanced.[7]

Alcohol Tolerance

If you're interested in natural tolerance, have a look at the previous chapter.[T] This section deals with the appealing prospect of acquiring or developing tolerance over time—the dream that whatever your natural gifts may be, you can still drink all your friends under the table—with a little hard work and dedication.

Is it possible? Absolutely.

The phenomenon of alcohol tolerance is very well documented. It has been successfully induced in mice and is easily observed in many college students during fraternity recruitment. Tolerance comes in a few varieties.[8]

With metabolic tolerance the body gets better at processing ethanol, so your BAC per unit of liquor consumed goes down. One study found an increase of between 30 and 80 percent in the rate of alcohol elimination in subjects who had been given ethanol regularly for a month.[9]

This improved rate of elimination is believed to be a consequence of additional enzyme production. While the majority of alcohol metabolism is handled by the enzyme alcohol dehydrogenase, the livers of regular drinkers adapt by stepping up production of cytochrome P450, another enzyme that can do the same job.[TT] Since alcohol dehydrogenase can process ethanol at only a limited, fixed rate, the presence of other reinforcements makes a big difference in how quickly you're able to get the booze out of your system.

There are also forms of tolerance that come into play even when BAC is the same. The body will try to adapt to the presence of ethanol and compensate where it can. That's not just if you're

Muscle, Weight, and Body Water, p. 123, Sex Differences in Metabolism, p. 124, Aging and Alcohol Consumption, p. 125

Ethanol Metabolism, p. 174

Blood Alcohol Concentration

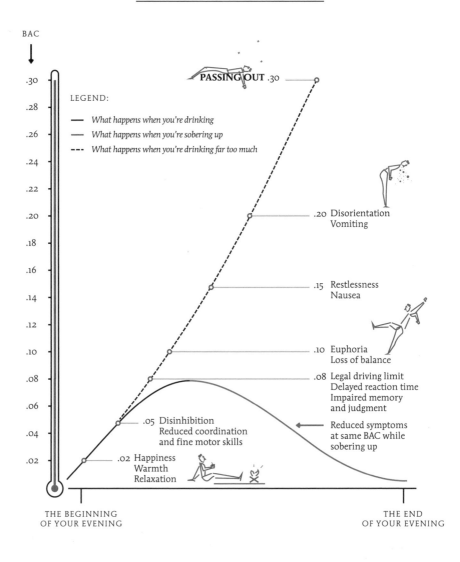

BAC

.30 **PASSING OUT** .30

LEGEND:

— What happens when you're drinking
— What happens when you're sobering up
--- What happens when you're drinking far too much

.28

.26

.24

.22

.20 _____ .20 Disorientation
Vomiting

.18

.16

.15 Restlessness
Nausea

.14

.12

.10 _____ .10 Euphoria
Loss of balance

.08 _____ .08 Legal driving limit
Delayed reaction time
Impaired memory
and judgment

.06

.05 Disinhibition   ← Reduced symptoms
Reduced coordination   at same BAC while
and fine motor skills   sobering up

.04

.02 Happiness
Warmth
Relaxation

THE BEGINNING   THE END
OF YOUR EVENING   OF YOUR EVENING

This graph shows rough outlines of what your blood alcohol level might look like over the course of a given night. Remember that your BAC depends on everything from how much muscle you have to whether you've eaten fruit recently—you can predict it in only a general and relative way.

a heavy, regular drinker, either: your body can acquire a measure of tolerance in a single drinking session.

This temporary tolerance is called the Mellanby effect, after the scientist who first identified it almost one hundred years ago. At a given blood alcohol level, people will invariably perform better on a sobriety test administered while their BAC is falling than one given while it's rising. The body will do its best to adjust to however much ethanol you flood it with, so when the levels begin to come back down, you're over-prepared to deal with what's left. (It's the same principle as training for a race by running twice as far.)[10]

There's also the fact that you probably aren't as drunk as you think you are most of the time.[T] If you've ever suddenly had to do something very important while blitzed (file a police report, say), you may have felt really sober really fast. Your blood alcohol concentration doesn't meaningfully change in the space of those few minutes, but the psychological effects of drinking dissipate rapidly.

Psychological Influences on Intoxication, p. 121

This may be why a pot of coffee or a cold shower often makes people feel more sober: it shakes them out of the "I'm drunk right now" mental space. Keep in mind, though, that these old remedies don't do anything about the alcohol in your bloodstream or your digestive system. If someone is clearly given over to the physiological effects of drinking—passed out, say—that shower will get them cold and wet but accomplish nothing else.

Still, there's a lot to be said for the mind's ability to overcome its own contributions to intoxication. In one experiment on alcohol tolerance, several groups were given both a drink and a task to complete. The group that was offered a reward for performing at sober levels while intoxicated outperformed all the others, showing signs of tolerance while their competition did not.[11]

If you really want to boost your tolerance and everything I've said still isn't enough for you, try hitting the gym. Higher muscle mass provides more places for the ethanol to diffuse to and a

Y
*Muscle,
Weight, and
Body Water,
p. 123*

lower BAC.[T] And it may make your body less angry about all that drinking.

Measuring Intoxication

How drunk you *were* is a topic for idle chitchat on a Sunday morning. How drunk you *are*, on the other hand, can be a deadly serious question. Your level of intoxication can have legal ramifications in the short term and life-altering consequences in the long term. Measuring it accurately is important. So how do we do that?

To determine impairment, what you need most is a picture of the alcohol levels in the brain. That is, after all, where effects like delayed reaction time take place.

Direct measurement of brain alcohol is an impractical proposition, to say the least—imagine a police officer whipping out a transcranial needle during a traffic stop—so we use proxies. Blood alcohol concentration, commonly abbreviated BAC, is the most reliable.

You may have heard the term *blood-brain barrier*, perhaps in reference to prescription drugs. Getting medicine into the blood is easy but getting it into the brain can be quite difficult. The brain, not unreasonably, has a protective layer to keep foreign chemicals out.

Because the brain's boundary is fatty, it's particularly effective at keeping water-based substances out. But ethanol mixes with everything, and it passes easily into the brain, which is one of the reasons it's popular as a recreational drug.[12]

It's also good news for your roadside stop, because it means BAC is a really effective proxy for your brain alcohol level. But police officers don't take a blood sample when they pull you over, either—they measure your breath alcohol content, or BrAC, and use it as a proxy for the proxy.

Studies done in the middle of the twentieth century gave an average BrAC to BAC ratio of one to twenty-one hundred

Police Stop

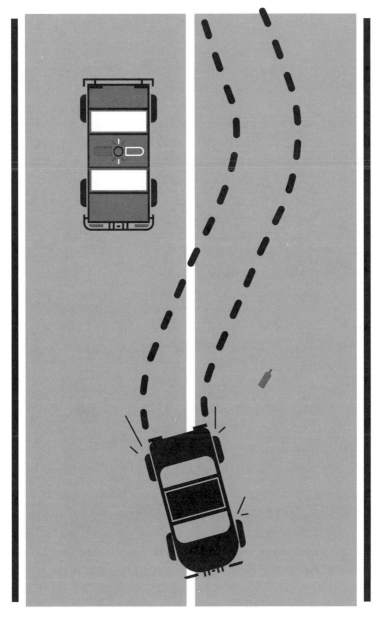

Don't drink and drive, friends.

(1:2100). That is, there's about the same amount of alcohol in a tenth of a liter of blood as there is in 210 liters of exhaled air. A Breathalyzer measures the latter and converts the reading to the former.[13]

This doesn't account for tolerance, in particular acute tolerance due to the Mellanby effect,[T] but there's a bigger issue at play: the twenty-one hundred conversion factor doesn't hold for everybody. Some people release relatively more or relatively less alcohol vapor through their lungs than the average.

One British study found a range of conversion values from eleven hundred to thirty-one hundred, depending on the individual and how far along he or she was in metabolizing the booze. A Croatian team found that fifteen minutes after a drink, converting BrAC measurements gave values nearly four times higher than directly testing the BAC did.[14]

In other words, a BAC of .08—the legal driving limit in the United States—is a benchmark, and not in any way a perfect one. But it's still the law, and in many places, the legal limit is defined in terms of both BAC and BrAC, and the police can book you if either one is too high.[15]

So please, for my sake and yours, if you get pulled over, don't try to explain to the cop how testing your breath alcohol is a poor proxy for how drunk you actually are. If you're drunk enough to think that will work, you shouldn't be driving anyhow.

Alcohol
Tolerance,
p. 137

Alcohol as Nutrient

In addition to its other properties, ethanol is a form of energy storage, good for about seven calories per gram. That's more than you'll get from proteins and carbohydrates but less than you'll get from fats.

Social drinkers get, on average, about a tenth of their total caloric intake from ethanol. For alcoholics, it can be as much as half, which has some interesting consequences.

First of all, the body hasn't got a good way to store ethanol energy. If you're a heavy enough drinker, your body will adapt and waste a lot of those booze calories. One study gave alcoholics a daily diet of twenty-five hundred calories in food and then added another two thousand in booze, and the subjects showed virtually no weight gain.[16]

Dieters shouldn't get too excited about the seemingly negligible impact of booze calories, though: it works this way only if you're drinking at a very high level. For the rest of us, seven calories is still seven calories. If you're drinking vodka, they're empty calories, to boot; if you're drinking beer, you'll get some actual vitamins and nutrients out of the deal, but you're also getting caloric carbohydrates and proteins in addition to the ethanol.

And if you are drinking at that heavy a level, you're going to run into a whole other set of problems. The liver ordinarily derives its energy from fats, but it burns ethanol preferentially if it's available. That leaves fats to accumulate in the liver, the first step on the long and decidedly unpleasant road to cirrhosis.

Alcoholics also tend to eat less, to eat more irregularly, and to have higher odds of malnutrition and vitamin A deficiencies in particular. That probably won't come as a surprise—nobody ever said a bar-food diet was healthy.

Dehydration

It's widely accepted that alcohol consumption leads to dehydration. You may even have heard that alcohol is a diuretic—that is, something that encourages urination. But how does it do this? Fortunately, this is an easy one.

The relevant organs here are the kidneys. If you don't know what they do, "make urine" is a good place to start. The kidneys are a repository for toxins and waste products from the blood. They also absorb water, which dissolves these unwanted chemicals, and then pass the mixture along to the bladder for excretion.

The kidneys have mechanisms in place to regulate how much water they're sending to the bladder and how much they're hanging onto. If you've tried wringing out a kitchen sponge with varying degrees of force, you know generally how this works.

A hormone called vasopressin regulates this process. Its entire job is to make the kidneys retain water: the more vasopressin in your system, the less water will make it to your bladder—and the less often you'll have to pee.

Alcohol inhibits vasopressin production, which gives the kidneys free rein to flood the bladder. The effects of this vasopressin suppression can start as little as twenty minutes after you begin drinking. You can lose a lot of water this way—four drinks' worth of booze can end up taking a quart of water out of your system.

If you drink enough, you can also get dehydrated by sweating, vomiting, or having diarrhea, but I don't recommend it.

Vasodilation, Heart Rate, and Heat Loss

You may have heard that alcohol is a vasodilator. Or you may not have heard that but recognize the word—prescription vasodilators are often given to people with high blood pressure and heart trouble. Simply put, a vasodilator causes your blood vessels to open wider than they normally would.

The walls of your veins and arteries are muscular and, like ordinary muscle tissue, they can contract and relax. Ethanol prompts them to do the latter, which opens up the passageways.

The mechanism by which this takes place is not fully understood, but the effect is very real. According to one study, whiskey was even more effective at vasodilation than some drugs prescribed for that purpose (although the dose required to maintain vasodilation was significant).[17]

The consequences of a drink are pretty clear, though. To begin with, your blood pressure will drop when your blood vessels expand, and your heart rate will increase. Think about it: when the container gets bigger, the liquid has more room to spread out and reduce its pressure; when the pressure drops, the pump needs to work harder for the same result. After a little while, these effects will reverse themselves.

Of particular consequence is the expansion of blood vessels in your skin—*cutaneous vasodilation* being the technical term for this phenomenon. It's responsible for ethanol's thermal effects on the body.

The circulatory system is a remarkable apparatus for temperature regulation. Your core tends to warm up your blood. If the core is too hot, the blood vessels in your skin dilate so that more heat can escape; when the blood returns to your core, it acts as a cooling agent. On the other hand, if it's too cold, those same vessels contract to retain more heat and keep your internal temperature from dropping too low.

The thing is, your skin is sensitive to temperature, too. As all that hot blood concentrates in your cutaneous blood vessels, and the heat dissipates across your skin, you'll begin to feel as if it's getting hotter. This is where that booze-induced warm feeling comes from, which is funny, because it actually means your core temperature is dropping.

In other words: you should not, under any circumstances, drink to warm up before you go out in the cold. You're just increasing your odds of hypothermia. Save the drinking for when you're back at the ski lodge.

Flush

Your face is beet red. You may be embarrassed, overheated, or just plain drunk. What's going on?

Ordinary flushing is a consequence of vasodilation, the body's natural cooling mechanism, whereby the blood vessels in the skin expand to maximize heat loss. You may notice your skin flushing when you eat hot or spicy food,[T] after exercise, on a hot

"Hot" and "Cool" Pseudo-Flavors, p. 105

day, or when you have a fever. Ethanol and certain other drugs act as vasodilators, with the same consequences.[†]

†
Vasodilation, Heart Rate, and Heat Loss, p. 144

This blood vessel expansion happens across the body, but it tends to be particularly noticeable in the face. The explanation for this is quite simple: the blood vessels in the cheeks are relatively large and less obscured than the ones in other parts of the body (they can't exactly be buried deep—your cheeks are only so thick).

I've called this phenomenon "ordinary flushing," above, but there is also an extraordinary type specific to one demographic—people of East Asian descent.

To explain this, we've got to review alcohol metabolism a little bit.[††] It's a two-step process, in which an enzyme called alcohol dehydrogenase turns ethanol into acetaldehyde, and then another enzyme, aldehyde dehydrogenase, turns the acetaldehyde into harmless acetate. There's a variety of different versions of each enzyme, and not everybody produces the same ones.

††
Ethanol Metabolism, p. 174

People of East Asian descent are doubly unlucky here (or possibly doubly lucky, but we'll get to that in a minute), because their populations have much higher rates of a gene that leads to very efficient alcohol dehydrogenase *and* higher rates of a different gene that leads to very inefficient aldehyde dehydrogenase. Each of these traits increases the time that acetaldehyde spends in the system.

Acetaldehyde is really rough on the body. It's an irritant, for a start; topical exposure can cause a rash, and getting it in your eyes is a great way to get conjunctivitis. A high level of the stuff in your blood is not something your body likes, which is why people who experience a strong flush reaction are also more likely to characterize intoxication as unpleasant. Acetaldehyde's effects are like the non-intoxicating parts of drinking on steroids: heart palpitations, lightheadedness, dizziness, warmth, and, of course, turning red due to vasodilation.[18]

Where's that good news I promised? Ineffective aldehyde dehydrogenase is thought to be a deterrent to alcohol abuse, because of all the unpleasant side effects. There's even a drug, called disulfiram, that's used to treat alcoholics by inhibiting this very enzyme. One could argue that people with this variant enzyme structure are naturally inoculated against alcoholism—and, in fact, that's the going theory for how the trait was selected.

Unfortunately, people who ignore that built-in warning and drink heavily anyway are at much higher risk for esophageal cancer, which is lethal in a majority of cases. Like I said, acetaldehyde is nasty.

Is Alcohol a Depressant or a Stimulant?

If you're like me, when you drink you get excited and friendly. You want to go out and do things, meet people, and have conversations. It's an active drug. But scientific types call it a depressant—and, we'll concede, we've all known (or been) the solitary, introspective drunk from time to time. What, exactly, is going on here?

It probably won't surprise you to know that the answer is *a lot*, beginning with the highly psychological aspects of intoxication. We assume ethanol will affect us in a certain way, and begin behaving accordingly before it has any physiological effect. It does stand to reason that differing expectations would lead to differing results—or, put another way, that drinking your way through a bachelor party doesn't feel the same as drinking away your sorrows.

Psychological Influences on Intoxication, p. 121

A team at the University of Chicago studied ethanol's stimulating and sedative effects in forty-nine social drinkers. From the point at which peak blood alcohol concentration was reached and onward, alcohol was a sedative for everybody. It was also a sedative for half the group on the way to that peak, while it was a stimulant for the other half.[19]

It's been known for some time that ethanol can have a stimulating effect, particularly early on in the consumption process. The most widespread theory about why this may be is that it prompts a release of dopamine, which is involved in the body's regulation of reward and desire (sound familiar?), and is also triggered by stimulants.

Researchers have also shown that the mere anticipation of ethanol can lead to increased dopamine levels. Granted, that was in rats, but don't tell me you've never felt a little disinhibited from the moment you sat down at the bar.[20]

Now, what about that whole depressant thing? Keep in mind that it doesn't mean alcohol makes you sad; it's more like a heavy blanket gets placed over your nervous system functions.

Ethanol enhances the effects of gamma-aminobutyric acid (you may forget that term immediately), generally referred to as GABA for convenience (you may want to remember that acronym). Ironically, GABA is your body's natural buzzkill—its job is to keep your neurons from getting more exited than they should.

Neuron excitement has nothing to do with how excited you feel but rather with the communication within your central nervous system. Ethanol-enhanced GABA activity gets in the way of your body's normal communications, slowing them down and leading to things like delayed reaction time.[21]

So the short answer is that ethanol is both a stimulant and a depressant, depending on who you are, where you are in the drinking process, and what your expectations are that day; but medically it's still classified as a depressant, because ethanol's only universal effects are decidedly sedative.

Alcohol's Effects on Sleep

Ah, the nightcap. A charming old tradition it is, that nice, relaxing glass of something distilled to form the boundary between the struggles of the day and the welcome embrace of sleep. It's also a ritual that fewer and fewer people will admit to performing (whether its prevalence is actually falling off or not), perhaps because it's so strongly associated with the ubiquitous casual alcoholism of the last century.

You have probably noticed that it's really easy to conk out when you've been drinking heavily. But, what's the prognosis for booze as a sleep aid, really? Very decidedly mixed.

First, the good news: alcohol does seem to help you fall asleep, at least a little. The time between lying down and dozing off is called "sleep latency," and a single drink consumed between thirty and sixty minutes before going to sleep appears to help you down the road to some z's. It makes sense, given that alcohol tends to slow down the central nervous system's communications, that it would help you relax into a snooze.[22]

That's about where the good news ends, though. Your body adapts to ethanol's sedative effects by trying to get your neurons more excited than they normally are, and those compensations are still in place once it has metabolized the booze. This leads to an increase in the likelihood that you'll wake up in the middle of the night, or at least not sleep as well as you otherwise might.[23]

The group of people for whom this rule of disrupted sleep does not apply is insomniacs. If you consistently have trouble falling or staying asleep, or wake up after adequate sleep without feeling rested—and it can't be attributed to stress, recreational or prescription drug use, life circumstances, or a mental-health condition—you may have an insomnia disorder, and alcohol will actually probably help you get as much deep sleep in a night as a healthy person your age. But you probably already knew that—a third of insomniacs admit to having tried drinking a nightcap to help them get to sleep, and two-thirds of those who've tried it say that it worked.[24]

Bottom line: alcohol may help you fall asleep, but it'll mess with your ability to actually get rested. Unless you're a diagnosed insomniac, in which case, go to town.

Is Alcohol a Depressant or a Stimulant?, p. 147

Alcohol's Effects on Sex

Lechery, sir, it provokes, and unprovokes; it provokes the desire, but
it takes away the performance.
—William Shakespeare, *Macbeth*, Act II, Scene 3

The Bard had it pretty much right. As we might put it today, drinking gives you "whiskey dick"—not quite as eloquent, but it does get points for assonance.

Alcohol affects the body's hormone levels in ways that tend to stimulate sexual interest; but it's also a sedative, which means that the intense nervous-system activity that normally goes into sex is at least somewhat dampened.

Let's start with the obvious: chronic alcohol abuse absolutely raises a man's odds of erectile dysfunction (ED). A study at one rehab center found that three-quarters of the patients experienced ED. Chronic users also experienced higher instances of premature ejaculation, reduced sexual desire, and difficulty achieving orgasm (presumably not all in the same guy). In other words, if you have any of these problems, you can always try the old "it's-not-you-baby-I'm-just-an-alcoholic" approach, but I'd find it a little worrisome if it succeeds.[25]

There's some good news here, too: the likelihood of sexual dysfunction as a simple result of drinking, rather than acute or chronic abuse, tends to be overestimated. One study of young, moderate drinkers found that about the worst thing that happens at a .08 BAC is that it takes a little longer to get an erection, and that even at .10 the negative effects were relatively mild. If you've had whiskey dick, there's a good chance you had a higher BAC or possibly psyched yourself out. The powers of suggestion are really strong when it comes to ethanol.[26]

Y
Psychological
Influences on
Intoxication,
p. 121

As for increased desire, one explanation is offered by the "myopia theory" of intoxication. This hypothesis holds that intoxication narrows the list of things we're able to pay attention to at once, which necessarily means that certain strong inputs get privileged. It's a straightforward enough theory, that maps onto lived experience pretty well and could explain everything from drunken fistfights to why greasy late-night food never tastes as good when you're sober and can think about the consequences.[27]

In a world where only the loudest signals are going to get through, sex is very likely to be one of them. It's hard to ignore visceral feelings of arousal, even and perhaps especially when you're blowing a .28 and can't feel anything else.

Drinking before sex seems to be less of a mixed bag for women. Studies have shown that it leads to decreased physiological arousal—measured by things like vaginal blood flow and time to orgasm. But it turns out that we're really bad at measuring physiological arousal in women anyway, and it tends not to correlate with subjective experience even in women who are stone-cold sober.[28]

Let's focus on the things we do know how to study. First, alcohol stimulates testosterone production in women. We think of testosterone as the masculinity hormone, which is a fair description, but it's also an arousal hormone (which, incidentally, tells us something about why adolescent boys are the way they are).

This increase in testosterone probably explains why higher BAC correlates with higher self-reported arousal and orgasmic pleasure in women. What's interesting is that self-reported arousal is also enhanced in women who are given placebos when expecting alcohol, particularly those who believe that alcohol makes sex better, and in both women and men who are drinking without realizing it.

It's pretty clear that drunken arousal is a result of both expectation and physical processes. This is particularly true at lower blood alcohol levels; the sedative effects of ethanol begin to predominate once you get above the legal limit.

Both men and women rate members of the opposite sex as more attractive when they've had a few. That may explain, at least partially, why alcohol consumption also leads to higher rates of next-morning regrets—which it definitely does, if you had any doubt—but let's remember that intoxication also raises your odds of potentially regrettable things like sleeping with strangers, failing to use contraception, and contracting venereal diseases.

Still not feeling guarded enough about drinking and sex? Here's a good one: it turns out people are even less likely to use a condom while drunk if they *think* that alcohol will make them less likely to use a condom. That's right, expectation can cut both ways.

Alcohol's Effects on Memory

The blackout: it's so common that there's a whole world of jokes and tongue-in-cheek terminology surrounding it. A present but spotty collection of memories is a "brownout," a sudden return to cognizance is "blacking in," and a camera is "how I remember my nights."

Blacking out is a form of anterograde amnesia, which is the medical term for being unable to form new long-term memories. It's distinct from retrograde amnesia, which wipes away previously formed memories and is more common on daytime television than in bars.

Researchers distinguish two types of blackouts: fragmentary, corresponding to the brownout described above; and en bloc, a continuous period when you might be talking, going places, even having sex, none of which you'll remember in the morning.[29]

You will remember what you're up to for a little while, though, which is one of the most interesting things about the en bloc blackout. One study found that people in a full blackout could retain memories for about two minutes, which is probably why blackouts aren't scary while you're having them: you've always got two minutes' worth of explanation for where you are and what you're doing.[30]

To black out, your blood alcohol concentration needs to exceed a certain threshold—something in the .30 range will give you at least an even chance, though blackouts have been documented at as little as .14 BAC. But it's the speed of consumption that seems to have the biggest impact on whether or not you'll remember your night.

The body has lots of mechanisms in place to adapt to all the booze you're pouring into it. (I feel like I've said this a lot.)ᵀ And it says a great deal about the body's capabilities that blackouts aren't a hard-ceiling phenomenon; if you really want to hang out at four times the legal limit without forgetting your evening, take it slow and you just might succeed. Though I feel obliged to add that this is neither a healthy nor a pleasant way to pass your time. *Please do not try this at home (or anywhere else).*

The fact that speed matters probably explains why doing shots and playing drinking games correlate with blacking out, as does the gulping of drinks—or drinking on an empty stomach. If you don't want to black out, having dinner and skipping the bourbon pong is a good way to start. (You may find useful advice on this subject in the previous chapter.)ᵀᵀ

You're also more likely to black out if you've done so before, though there's an ongoing debate about why. One explanation is that some people are simply more prone to blacking out to begin with, so that first time was basically inevitable once they started drinking a certain way. An alternative hypothesis suggests that your first blackout damages your brain in a way that makes it susceptible to repeated memory impairment in the future.

Well, that escalated quickly. Any chance we can stick with the former explanation? I'd say we might—a major study of one hundred hospitalized alcoholics found that a third of them had *never* blacked out. Surely the brains of social drinkers, blackout or no, are less pickled than an actual alcoholic's?

Meanwhile, a study of college students found that half the ones who drank had experienced at least one blackout. So even if you have done some damage experimenting with anterograde amnesia, you're in pretty good company.[31]

Y
Drinking Speed, p. 112, *Alcohol Tolerance,* p. 137, *Measuring Intoxication,* p. 140

YY
Drinking Speed, p. 112, *Food Intake,* p. 114

Hangover

Greetings, gentle reader! If you are reading this when it's early in the morn—er, afternoon—and the sun is far too bright and your head feels like a watermelon with a subwoofer inside, I'm sorry to say I can't offer you an easy, one-stop cure. If I could, believe me, I'd have gone and gotten a patent instead of writing this book. But some of what follows may be helpful or at least distracting. (Readers who are looking this over before they really need it: well done! I may be of more use to you.)

Hangovers are complicated, messy, and extremely unpleasant. You may feel sick to your stomach, a consequence of ongoing spins[T] and the chemical irritant you insisted on pouring into your stomach all night. You probably didn't get enough sleep.[TT] You are almost certainly dehydrated,[TTT] which contributes to a general malaise and definitely won't help your inevitable headache.

Oh, and to make matters worse, you may still have booze in your system. Ethanol is eliminated at a fixed rate,[TTTT] so depending on how long it has been since you stopped drinking, your liver may still have some work to do. Meanwhile, your stomach passes its contents along more slowly if you've eaten, so you may still have some rum-soaked late-night Chinese food in there come morning.

If you've been drinking heavily, you've been filling your body with poisons, and I don't even mean the booze itself. Ethanol's metabolite, acetaldehyde, is something that not one single tissue in your body likes to touch. And if you've been drinking anything other than the purest vodka, you may have accumulated undesirable fermentation leftovers as well. You may have heard these referred to as "congeners"; they're a convenient scapegoat for hangovers because they're hard to tally in a given drink and their interplay is even harder to assess.

The list of plausible congeners includes things like methanol, ethanol's toxic, blinding cousin,[TTTTT] and there is some evidence to support congeners' role in causing hangovers. Bour-

[T] *Imbalance and the Spins, p. 134*

[TT] *Alcohol's Effects on Sleep, p. 148*

[TTT] *Dehydration, p. 143*

[TTTT] *Ethanol Metabolism, p. 174*

[TTTTT] *Methanol, p. 47*

Symptoms of a Hangover

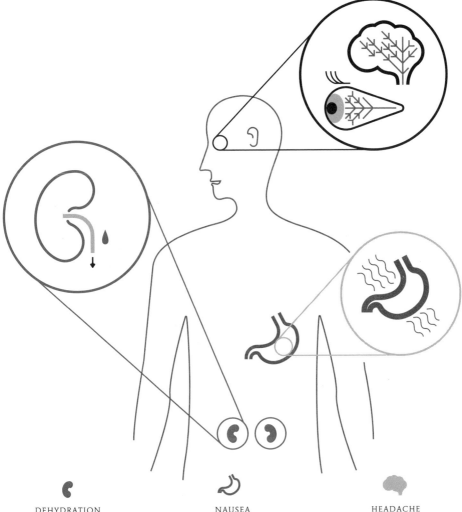

DEHYDRATION

The kidneys normally retain water, but alcohol inhibits the hormone that tells them to; it all goes straight to the bladder instead. This is why you need the bathroom more often when you're drinking—and why you'll wake up feeling dehydrated.

NAUSEA

Ethanol is a chemical irritant: essentially, it tickles your membranes in exactly the wrong way. If you have a lot to drink, there may still be some in your stomach throughout the night, irritating the lining and making you want to throw up in the morning.

HEADACHE

The hangover headache is generally attributed to vasodilation: as blood vessels expand, they put pressure on tissues inside the skull. You may get some relief by consuming a vasoconstrictor, like caffeine.

bon, for instance, contains methanol in nearly seven times the concentration found in vodka and is almost twice as likely to cause hangovers. One study found that vodka and pure ethanol caused mild headaches, but any spirit at least as complex as gin (which is really a particular class of flavored vodka) led to true hangover symptoms.[32] The body also preferentially metabolizes ethanol, which means the methanol can stay in your system much longer before being processed into its symptom-causing metabolites—consistent with the fact that you don't usually feel hungover until you've at least paused in your drinking.

Speaking of pauses, some effects of the hangover are thought to be mild withdrawal symptoms. Your body adapts rapidly enough to the presence of alcohol that you're soberer at a given BAC on the way down than you were at the same BAC on the way up (called the "Mellanby effect").[Y] The body answers generalized nervous system depression with increased activity; when the depressant is gone, those elevated levels remain, giving you symptoms like the morning hand tremor. Ordinarily these effects dissipate in a matter of hours, if you even notice them, but chronic heavy drinkers and people who hit the sauce *way* too hard in one sitting may find withdrawal symptoms lingering for multiple days.

The truth is, hangovers are complicated and probably reflect a variety of concurrent phenomena. The headache, for instance, is ubiquitous enough to show up even in the absence of congeners, but we're not quite sure why. A common—and totally plausible—explanation is that it's a consequence of vasodilation:[YY] if the blood vessels in your head expand, they put pressure on tissues that aren't used to it. If that's the cause, having a cup of coffee isn't a bad idea. Caffeine is a vasoconstrictor, so it should treat the problem directly; and there's even some evidence that caffeine counteracts the hangover headache in rats. (Yes, apparently we can measure how much rats' heads hurt.)[33]

But there's so much more to how liquor affects the body, and we're barely scratching the surface. Ethanol stimulates the pro-

Y
Alcohol Tolerance, p. 137

YY
Vasodilation, Heart Rate, and Heat Loss, p. 144

duction of prostaglandins, which seem pretty clearly to contribute to the morning-after feeling: people given a prostaglandin inhibitor called tolfenamic acid before drinking had reduced hangover symptoms across the board and a reduced headache in particular. Oh, and prostaglandins are also vasodilators, just to add to the recursive confusion.[34]

Still hoping for a cure? The best I can offer is all stuff you'll have heard before, much of it preventative: don't drink too much, too fast, or on an empty stomach; if you're prone to harsh hangovers, stick to clear spirits; drink a lot of water; get adequate sleep; and consider taking ibuprofen or aspirin, which are also prostaglandin inhibitors, if you've got a nasty headache.

And if you've got some money lying around, please: fund more studies in search of a hangover cure. Hangovers are estimated to cost the United States $148 billion every year in lost productivity alone. I shudder to think what that number must be in Russia.

Hair of the Dog That Bit You

If you've read the previous section, you've probably come to the conclusion that the "hair of the dog" remedy—that is, curing a hangover by drinking more—will not help. That is overwhelmingly, but not completely, true. Allow me to present the pros and the cons:

Pros

→ If part of the problem is poisoning by methanol's toxic metabolite, formaldehyde, adding more ethanol will delay the body's metabolism of the methanol. Note: that's *delay* and not *prevent*.

→ If part of the problem is withdrawal from ethanol, adding more will lessen withdrawal symptoms. Note: that's *lessen* and not *eliminate*. Also, "I need more of this drug to get me through the withdrawal" is probably not something you want to catch yourself saying.

Cons

⟶ If your stomach is irritated, another drink will irritate it even more.

⟶ If you're dehydrated, it will dehydrate you even more.

⟶ If your blood vessels are dilated, it will dilate them even more.

⟶ Literally any ethanol-induced symptom you're experiencing other than withdrawal will probably be made worse and extended further into the day by adding more.

The best case to be made for the hair of the dog is that it puts you back into drinking mode, which most people find preferable to hangover mode. After a night of hard drinking, your body is at least somewhat calibrated to being awash in ethanol; filling it up again feels better than running on booze fumes. But unless you plan to spend the rest of your life buzzed, you will *eventually* need to recalibrate back to normal sober functioning, and the hangover is the price you'll pay.

A Nightcap

Alcohol Consumption in Animals

This book has focused on drinking in just three sorts of creatures: yeast, bacteria, and humans. There's good reason for that: these microbes make the booze, and most of my readers who drink it are, I assume, human. But we're not nature's only creations to have a relationship with ethanol—far from it.

Let's start with our closest relatives. Chimpanzees, like humans' perennial teenage cousins, are less advanced than we are in their drinking but impressively resourceful in getting a buzz going. They're fans of palm wine, the naturally fermenting sap of the palm tree, also enjoyed by many people across the world. It clocks in at about the strength of a beer.

Wild chimps make scoops and sponges out of leaves to get at the good stuff. The first scientific study of this phenomenon observed this behavior in West Africa over the course of seventeen years, finding that the drinking could be either social or solitary, that some individuals drank more—or more frequently—

than others, and that chimpanzees display such signs of intoxication as somnolence and agitation. Perhaps most important of all, this study provided hard evidence that ethanol consumption is a natural behavior and doesn't show up only when animals have been introduced to man-made alcohol products.[1]

On the other side of the world, the vervet monkeys of the Caribbean are famous for their love of a good drink. They're not satisfied with the products of natural fermentation, though—they prefer rum, mixed into tropical cocktails, and they like it so much they've been known to steal drinks from inattentive tourists at beach bars.[2]

Vervet monkeys have some other traits that might seem familiar. They drink most heavily as adolescents and sober up a bit as they get older. Females are more likely to imbibe moderately and to prefer sweeter drinks. Alcoholic vervets tend to like their drinks strong. Some will drink themselves unconscious or show signs of withdrawal if they're shut off. Females are more likely to imbibe moderately and to prefer sweeter drinks.

But it's not just primates that like an adult beverage, as much fun as the chimps and the vervets are. Some bears seem to have a taste for beer, though they need to consume quite a lot of it to really enjoy themselves. A family of Norwegian bears went through a hundred beers in a single bender back in 2012, in addition to gorging themselves on marshmallows and trashing the cabin in which they found all this stuff.

Another bear, in Washington State, went through thirty-six cans of beer before passing out. He had a clear brand preference, too. He evidently didn't care for Busch beer—after trying one can of it he declined to open another—but liked local favorite Rainier so much that the authorities used cans of it to trap him for transportation.[3]

It is commonly thought that elephants get drunk off naturally fermenting fruit, but that's almost certainly not true. Those drunken bears probably weighed a few hundred pounds each; an elephant is heavier by an order of magnitude, sometimes two. It would take a lot of dedication for a five-ton animal to get drunk on slightly fermented fruit.

What definitely can get elephants drunk, however, is the consumption of large amounts of man-made booze. Indian pachyderms are known to enjoy rice beer and go on the occasional drunken rampage. Ever broken something during a bender? Imagine the damage you'd do if you were a hundred times heavier and stronger.

Primates, elephants, and bears are just the tip of the ice cube. At least one Swedish moose has gotten drunk enough from fermented apples to get stuck in a tree. A feral pig in Australia knocked back eighteen beers before getting into a heated disagreement with a cow. There are stories of a pet rhinoceros in eighteenth-century Britain that liked the occasional glass of red wine, and in present-day Canada, a ranch is giving its beef cattle a liter of wine daily.

Insects get in on the game too. Butterflies sometimes find their way into beer cans, and certain butterfly species get loaded on fermenting fruit before settling in for the winter. (It's not entirely clear, at least to me, whether this latter behavior is intentional, or a consequence of dwindling supplies of non-fermented foods.) Drunken honeybees have trouble standing and tend to end up on their backs, and drinking also screws up their social behavior. Fruit flies can become alcoholics, will drink more if they haven't gotten laid recently, and, incidentally, definitely prefer vinegar to honey. ⵟ

Y
*Other
Fermenting
Agents,
p. 23*

A few species are famous for their tolerance. The pen-tailed treeshrew of Malaysia, for instance, enjoys a few nightly rounds of fresh palm wine, which occurs naturally in its habitat. It can drink the rough equivalent of nine drinks for a human without showing loss of coordination or other visible signs of intoxication. Not bad, right? Slow lorises also come to the treeshrews' party and leave without getting too buzzed, though that may be because they are larger and tend to spend much less time drinking. Meanwhile, Central American bats, after feeding on fermented fruit and nectar, can hit a BAC four times the legal driving limit without flying or echolocating any worse than they normally would.

Avian species, largely small and lightweight, don't need much to get plastered. A lot of birds like eating fruits and berries, which are potent natural sources of alcohol. European blackbirds, red-wings, and Bohemian waxwings have all been known to get very drunk in this manner, particularly during winter and especially when they're young.[4]

My favorite nonhuman drinker of all would have to be the zebra finch. Researchers in Oregon got a bunch of these little Australian songbirds buzzed, with BACs between .05 and .08, by putting a bit of ethanol and juice in their water bottles. The idea was to test how drinking affected the finches' singing. The drunken birds got a little quieter, and their musical patterns got a little muddled. In other words, just as you and I may slur our words when we get drunk, zebra finches slur their songs.[5]

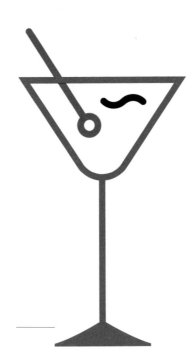

Resources

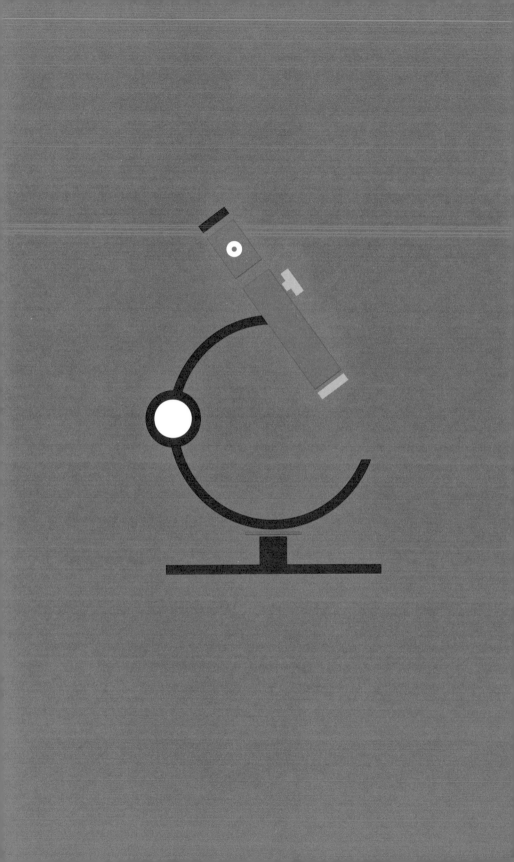

Appendix

Scientific Background

In the course of researching and writing this book, I found that a handful of important topics came up again and again. To make your reading easier, I've compiled here a quick and dirty rundown of a few of the most relevant background topics.

Vapor Pressure and Volatility

Possibly the most important topic when it comes to understanding the properties of alcohol described in this book, vapor pressure is also unhelpfully defined in most readily available resources. They usually tell you some story about the hypothetical pressure in a closed container, and you've forgotten what you were looking for by the end of the paragraph.

Vapor pressure is simply an indication of how volatile a liquid is—that is, how likely it is to release some of its particles as gaseous vapors. The pressure buildup in a closed container due to those vapors is the best measurement we have for that likelihood, and so it's our common shorthand for volatility.

A given liquid has different vapor pressures at different temperatures. This is why hot water evaporates faster than cold water does. Dial the temperature up and you reach the boiling point, which is where the liquid's vapor pressure—its tendency to move outward into the air—becomes equal to the atmospheric pressure pushing back on it.

This is, incidentally, why cooking times in Denver aren't the same as those in Boston. Water boils at a lower temperature at high altitudes because of the lower atmospheric pressure.

Got all that?

Because a particular substance's vapor pressure changes with temperature, it might not seem like a good general benchmark for volatility. Fortunately for us, the hierarchy of vapor pressures is pretty consistent: if one substance is more volatile than

Vapor Pressure

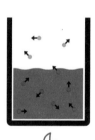 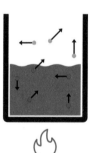

WATER	ETHANOL	METHANOL
At 148.5°, water is hot but not boiling. Some water molecules will evaporate from the surface and escape as water vapor; some of that vapor will also condense back into the liquid.	Ethanol is more volatile than water at the same temperature, so it evaporates more rapidly and condenses more slowly.	Methanol is more volatile than either water or ethanol and boils at 148.5°. Vaporization still happens at the surface, but now it also happens deep in the liquid, resulting in the formation of gas bubbles.

another at sea level, you can expect that still to be true at the bottom of Death Valley and the top of Mount Everest.

How does this connect to booze? It's how stills work, for a start: they rely on the fact that water, ethanol, and nasties like methanol all have different volatilities. The distillation process normally involves boiling one off while leaving (most of) the rest behind.

It's also an important component of smell, which is, in turn, an important component of taste. Your nose can tell what's in something because a few of its molecules have wafted up to make contact with your olfactory bulb. A more volatile substance will have a stronger smell. Distillers often refer to the aromatic chemicals in their spirits collectively as the "volatiles."

That volatility has another implication, of course, which is that scented things can wear out over time. It's true: if you leave a bottle of fine Scotch open on the counter, its flavor chemicals will evaporate, just as water does.

Ethanol as a Solvent

To continue our recap from high school chemistry, a solvent is a substance (for today, let's stick to liquids) in which something else can be dissolved. That something else is the solute. If you stir sugar into a glass of water, the sugar is the solute and the water is the solvent. Together, the two substances constitute a solution.

Things dissolve because the bonds holding their molecules together are broken and have trouble re-forming. A good solvent has to be effective at breaking those bonds and at preventing their restoration.

Ethanol is a useful solvent in some important ways: it mixes easily with water, for a start, but there are also things that dissolve more easily in ethanol than they do in water. Anethol, which is responsible for the ouzo effect, provides the most dramatic example of this.[Y]

Emulsions: Absinthe and Milk Punch, p. 85

Ethanol is also a very good carrier for those volatile aromatic chemicals that give an aged rum or whiskey its wonderful flavor. For the same reason, it's used in essential-oil extraction—a process not entirely unlike the extracting of flavor from juniper berries in gin making—and as the basis for colognes and perfumes.

Ethanol Digestion

Alcohol is absorbed into the blood by passive diffusion, which simply means it starts in an area of higher concentration (the intestines or stomach) and tries to spread to an area of lower concentration (the blood). The king of diffusion sites is the small intestine, with its thin walls and very high surface area. Its main purpose is to absorb nutrients into your bloodstream. If you're drinking on an empty stomach, 90 percent of your etha-

Membrane Diagram

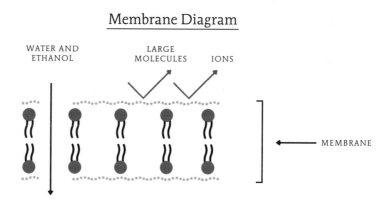

Cell membranes are made of lipid molecules. They have a central point that likes water a lot, as well as two long tails that really hate water and want to get as far away from it as possible; the result looks kind of like a bobby pin. Two rows of these lipids, facing in opposite directions, make up a membrane.

The water-loving outer surfaces of membranes carry an electric charge, which makes it hard for ions and polar molecules to get through. Uncharged molecules can also have trouble if they're too big. Cells have special mechanisms for admitting these types of molecules when necessary.

Water and ethanol, however, are small and not repelled by the charges at the membrane's surface. They can slip right between the lipid bobby pins, easily diffusing into all of the tissues in your body.

nol absorption will take place in the small intestine; with food, it drops down to 70 percent, because the ethanol spends more time in your stomach and a greater percentage of it gets absorbed there. Ethanol absorption in other locations is possible—the membranes of the human body are very permeable to the stuff—but virtually all of it is accounted for in the stomach and small intestine.

Liquor stays in your stomach longer with food because the stomach modulates the speed at which its contents move on to the small intestine. This is called the "gastric emptying rate," and it slows down when the stomach has extra work to do, like digesting a large amount of food.

The speed of gastric emptying affects not only the location of ethanol absorption but also the overall amount of absorption. The stomach contains alcohol dehydrogenase, the enzyme that metabolizes ethanol out of your system; the longer your drink hangs out in there, the less ethanol will be left when it reaches the intestine. This makes the gastric emptying rate one of the most important factors in determining how intoxicated you'll become.

Most of ethanol metabolism takes place in the liver. You may not think of your liver as connected to your digestive system—I certainly never used to—but it's the first stop your blood makes after loading up with nutrients at your small intestine. The liver's role is to screen your blood for poisons and toxic doses of otherwise useful chemicals before they arrive at your heart and get pumped out to the rest of the body.

The liver can produce alcohol dehydrogenase only so quickly. Above about a .02 BAC, you're adding ethanol to your blood faster than your body can get rid of it. This makes speed of consumption a major factor in your level of intoxication as well.

Now, let's zoom in on those processes taking place in the liver.

Ethanol Metabolism

Metabolism, simply put, is your body's transformation of one substance into another by means of an enzyme your body has produced. There are various reasons the body engages in these chemical modifications, like obtaining energy, making particular compounds it needs to grow and maintain itself, and neutralizing dangerous substances.

Ethanol is metabolized by the following enzymes and families of enzymes:

Enzyme	Pathway	Location*	Contribution
Alcohol Dehydrogenases	Oxidative	Liver and Stomach	Do the vast majority of the work under normal conditions
Cytochrome P450s	Oxidative	Liver	Relevant principally at very high ethanol concentrations
Catalase	Oxidative	Throughout the body	Very little, except when drinking in a fasting state
Phospholipidase D	Non-oxidative	Liver	Very little, except when drinking in a fasting state
Fatty Acids	Non-oxidative	Liver and Pancreas	Very little, unless oxidative pathways are blocked

*Trace amounts of all of these may be found in various types of cells throughout the body, but the work of metabolism takes place principally in the organs listed.

As any doctor, pharmacist, or biochemical researcher can tell you, this is all extremely complicated. If you want to read more on the topic, I recommend Samir Zakhari's overview for the National Institute on Alcohol Abuse and Alcoholism, appropriately titled "How Is Alcohol Metabolized by the Body?"

For the purposes of this book, we'll simplify by dealing exclusively with the three oxidative-pathway enzymes and almost entirely with alcohol dehydrogenase.

"Pathway" refers to the method by which the enzyme transforms ethanol into something else, and "oxidative" indicates that the method is an oxidation reaction. Oxidation reactions can be variously defined as reactions that add oxygen atoms to a substance, cause that substance to lose hydrogen atoms, or cause that substance to lose electrons. Don't sweat the details here. In the vast majority of situations, the ethanol in your body will be metabolized by oxidation stripping off two of its hydrogen atoms. The ethanol then goes from this:

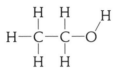

to this:

Acetaldehyde is nasty, nasty stuff. It's a known animal carcinogen and a suspected human one. If you got it on you, you'd feel a burning sensation. Your eyes would water and you'd start coughing. Your body doesn't want it in your blood.

Acetaldehyde, in turn, is metabolized by aldehyde dehydrogenase 2, in the course of which it's taken from this:

to this:

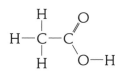

Acetate, the result, is not poisonous, and the body is quite used to dealing with it. I'll spare you the additional steps and say only that acetate passes through what's called the citric acid cycle, eventually getting converted into water, carbon dioxide, and energy.

That covers oxidative-pathway metabolism in general. Now, let's focus on alcohol dehydrogenase for a bit.

If you haven't consumed anything that inhibits alcohol dehydrogenase, have eaten in the last day, and aren't on the bender to end all benders, this enzyme will handle virtually all of your ethanol metabolism.

Alcohol dehydrogenase comes in a whole bunch of types, with catchy names like ADH1B*2, which are grouped into five major classes. They all have distinct properties. Some process alcohol more rapidly than others. Some tend to appear only in the liver, while others show up in multiple organs; ADH IV is pretty much confined to the stomach.

That variety matters, because not everybody produces the same set of enzymes at the same concentrations. Production varies by age, ethnicity, and sex—men tend to have higher levels of alcohol dehydrogenase in their stomachs than women do, as one example out of many.

A similar variation is true of aldehyde dehydrogenase, which helps your body get rid of acetaldehyde, and although the aldehyde dehydrogenase family is not quite as large, the differences among people may be even starker. The ALDH2*2 variant, common in East Asian populations, is much slower to eliminate acetaldehyde from the body than ALDH2*1 is; this is what accounts for the particularly strong flush reaction that certain people of East Asian descent experience while drinking.[T]

Ⓨ
Flush,
p. 145

Glossary

Beverages

absinthe, A high-proof spirit flavored with anise, wormwood, and other medicinal herbs. Generally served with sugar and a significant amount of water, resulting in the clouding effect described in Chapter 4.

ale, A variety of beer brewed at comparatively warm temperatures (above 60°F), with the result that a large number of fruity and floral esters are produced. Distinguished from the colder-brewed *lager*.

aquavit, A distilled spirit generally made from grains or potatoes and flavored with spices, especially caraway and dill. Primarily associated with Scandinavia.

bitters, A maceration of highly aromatic herbs and spices, usually in ethanol but occasionally in glycerin. *Cocktail bitters*, such as Angostura and Peychaud's, are meant to be used a few drops at a time as flavoring agents. They are also called *nonpotable bitters* to distinguish them from *potable bitters* like Campari, which are generally consumed in larger quantities.

bourbon, An American whiskey made from at least 51 percent corn. Strongly associated with and primarily produced in Kentucky, although it can be made anywhere in the United States. Bourbon is known as the smoother and sweeter of the two major American whiskey types.

brandy, A distillate of grapes, strongly associated with the wine-growing regions of the Mediterranean. Distillates of other fruits are also referred to as brandies, generally with the name of the fruit specified, as in *apple brandy, plum brandy, cherry brandy,* etc.

Champagne, A type of sparkling wine produced in the Champagne region of France. Traditionally undergoes a secondary fermentation in the bottle, after which the lees (sediment composed of dead yeast cells and other particles) are carefully removed, in a process called *disgorging,* before the bottle is sealed and sold.

Cognac, A type of brandy produced in France, in the vicinity of the town of Cognac, in accordance with strict rules. Traditionally produced in pot stills and aged in oak barrels for a period of years or decades, Cognacs are known for their smoothness and for their notes of fruit and caramel.

curacao, Originally, a liqueur made by infusing spirits with the peels of the laraha fruit, a bitter orange found on the Caribbean island of Curaçao; today may refer to any orange-flavored liqueur, irrespective of origin or production process. A popular blue variation has been available since the early 20th century.

gin, A distilled spirit ordinarily but not necessarily made from grains, flavored with various spices among which juniper is the most prominent. The flavoring process may involve infusion or flavor extraction in the course of distillation.

highball, A combination of hard liquor with a carbonated mixer, containing noticeably more of the latter. The highball category includes the Scotch and Soda, the Gin and Tonic, and the Dark and Stormy; regarding an individual drink, the term usually refers to a mixture of whiskey and soda water or ginger ale.

IPA, An abbreviation of *India pale ale,* a heavily hopped style of beer originally designed to survive the long voyage from Britain to India by taking advantage of hops' preservative powers. Known for being bitter and light and for a pronounced hops flavor.

lager, A variety of beer brewed at comparatively cool temperatures (below 60°F), with mild, subtle flavors and a low danger of off notes. Distinguished from the warmer-brewed *ale.*

lambic beer, A Belgian style of ale spontaneously fermented by wild yeasts and bacteria. Known for having fruity or "funky" flavors and for being quite sour.

liqueur, A flavored distilled beverage with added sugar, made by the infusion of fruits, spices, or other flavorings in a spirit. Ordinarily 20–30 percent alcohol by volume, although some may be much stronger. Liqueurs go by many other names in the United States, including *cordial, schnapps,* and *flavored brandy.*

Madeira, A fortified wine produced in the Madeira Islands, a

Portuguese territory off the African coast. May be fortified during or after fermentation, or both. Known today as a dessert wine.

ouzo, The distinctive spirit of Greece, produced by flavoring neutral grain spirits with anise and other spices. Known for becoming cloudy when water is added, in the same manner as absinthe.

port, A type of fortified wine made in Portugal, fortified with grape spirits before fermentation is complete, and then aged. Generally sweet and often served as a dessert wine.

prosecco, A type of sparkling wine produced in Italy. Traditionally undergoes a secondary fermentation in a pressurized stainless steel vat before being strained and bottled, in contrast to Champagne.

rum, A distillate of sugarcane or its by-products.

rye, An American whiskey style made from at least 51 percent rye. Rye is known as the rougher and spicier of the two major American whiskey types.

Scotch, An abbreviation of *Scotch whisky*. The distinctive spirit of Scotland, Scotch is made primarily from malted barley and is known for flavor notes of peat and smoke.

sherry, A type of fortified wine made in Spain, fortified with

grape spirits after fermentation. Traditionally aged using a *solera* method, in which new wine is added to aging casks as old wine is drawn off, resulting in a mixture of many ages.

stout, An abbreviation of *stout porter*; historically used to describe a particularly strong variety of porter beer. Today refers to very dark beers with a rich flavor and a thick or creamy consistency, in particular those made with roasted barley.

tequila, A distillate of blue agave, a succulent plant native to Mexico. Tequilas may be unaged, aged for a period of months, or aged for a period of years; labeled as *blanco*, *reposado*, or *añejo*, respectively.

vodka, A distillate of anything, most commonly potatoes or cereal grains, that has been distilled to the highest proof allowed by nature and then blended with water to a level fit for human consumption. Most strongly associated with the Slavic countries, vodka is as close to a pure mixture of ethanol and water as one can get. It is not aged.

whiskey, A distillate of cereal grains, most frequently barley, corn, rye, or wheat. Scotch whisky, Irish whiskey, bourbon, and rye are the most common varieties. *Whiskey* is the common spelling in the United States and Ireland, *whisky* in Canada and Scotland. Whiskeys are normally aged in oak barrels.

Terms

acetaldehyde, The aldehyde produced by the oxidation of ethanol, as occurs in the course of ethanol metabolism by alcohol dehydrogenase. An irritant and a probable carcinogen, it's blamed for many of drinking's less pleasant side effects. Present in small quantities in certain spirits, providing a grassy flavor note. Also called *ethanal*.

acetic acid, The distinctive flavor and primary non-water component of vinegar. Also the final output of human ethanol metabolism, produced when acetaldehyde is metabolized by aldehyde dehydrogenase.

acetone, A solvent, commonly used in paint thinners and nail-polish removers. Produced in harmless quantities during fermentation; concentrated in the heads of a distillation run and ordinarily discarded.

ADH, see *alcohol dehydrogenase*

alcohol by volume, The percentage of the volume of a given liquid that is ethanol; often abbreviated *ABV*. Generally between 5 percent and 15 percent for fermented drinks and in the neighborhood of 40 percent for hard liquor.

alcohol dehydrogenase, The primary enzyme involved in metabolizing ethanol and other alcohols; it works by oxidizing them into aldehydes. Found primarily in the liver and the stomach. Often abbreviated *ADH*.

aldehyde, A category of organic molecules distinguished by the presence of a formyl group, a carbon atom bonded to a hydrogen atom and double-bonded to an oxygen atom. Many flavors chemicals are aldehydes, including those characteristic of cinnamon and vanilla. Aldehydes can be produced by the oxidation of alcohols, and are intermediate by-products of human alcohol metabolism.

aldehyde dehydrogenase, The primary enzyme involved in metabolizing aldehydes; works by oxidizing them into carboxylic acids. Often abbreviated *ALDH*.

ALDH, see *aldehyde dehydrogenase*

amygdala, A part of the brain involved in memory and emotional associations, both of which are strongly tied to the sense of smell, due to its direct connection to the olfactory bulb.

anterograde amnesia, An inability to form new long-term memories, resulting in a period of time that one is unable to recall. Alcohol-induced blackouts are the most familiar example. Distinguished from *retrograde amnesia*, in which memories previously formed are lost, and which is more commonly associated with physical injuries.

anthocyanin, A class of phenolic pigments known for providing the color of red wine.

astringent, Causing a drying or puckering sensation in the mouth. Associated with red wines and distilled spirits in general, and with tannins in particular. An important component of mouthfeel.

blood alcohol concentration, A measurement of the ethanol level in the blood, often abbreviated *BAC.* In the United States, BAC is measured in grams of ethanol per deciliter of blood, with 1g/dL being expressed as a BAC of .1 (or .10). A BAC of .08 is often treated as the turning point between mostly psychological drunkenness and mostly physiological drunkenness and is consequently the legal threshold for driving while intoxicated. Higher BACs tend to correlate with memory impairment, risky behavior, nausea, and loss of consciousness; a BAC of .3 or higher carries a risk of death. BAC may also be called *blood alcohol content, blood alcohol level, blood ethanol concentration,* and all permutations of these.

carboxylic acid, A category of organic molecules distinguished by the presence of a carboxyl group, a carbon atom bonded to a hydroxyl group (an oxygen atom attached to a hydrogen atom) and double-bonded to another oxygen atom. Produced by the oxidation of aldehydes.

Acetic acid and formic acid are both carboxylic acids.

casein, A type of protein found in milk and other dairy products. Used as a fining agent in wine.

cellulose, A class of organic chemicals that form the fibrous structural framework of wood and green plants. Consists of long chains of sugars (longer than those in hemicellulose) so tightly packed as to be indigestible; some sugars are released by burning, producing flavors like those of caramel, which are absorbed into spirits aging in charred or toasted barrels.

cirrhosis, A deterioration of the liver, generally caused by a buildup of fat, hepatitis B or C, or long-term alcohol abuse. It's often used metonymically to convey all the deadly consequences of alcoholism.

congener, In the sense used in this book, a chemical component of a hard liquor other than water or ethanol. Most often refers to those chemicals believed to cause or worsen hangovers, although the term technically also covers pigments and desirable flavors.

cooperage, The practice of barrel-making; a barrel-making business. A person engaged in this profession is a *cooper.*

cytochrome P450, A class of enzyme heavily involved in metabolizing drugs in the body. Known to be inhibited by certain substances, including grapefruit, which can result in dangerously high concentrations of affected drugs in the blood.

decant, To pour a liquid from one vessel to another. Decanting is particularly associated with wine, in which context it may be used to separate the wine from its sediment, affect its flavor by aeration and exposure to atmospheric oxygen, or simply enhance the aesthetic experience of wine-drinking by moving the wine from a bottle into a sometimes ornate vessel, called a *decanter.*

diacetyl, One of the distinctive flavor components of butter and of "buttery" Chardonnays.

disinhibition, A state or feeling of being free from the constraints we would otherwise place on our behavior, usually in the context of intoxication. The common explanation for why we act the way we do when we're drunk.

distillation, The separation of the liquids in a mixture, most often by heating it and recondensing the vapors that boil off. The device used for this is called a *still.* See Chapter 2.

dopamine, A chemical produced by the body, involved in the regulation of reward and desire. Its production is stimulated by the consumption—and possibly by the expectation—of ethanol.

endorphin, A class of chemical produced by the body to reduce the sensation of pain. A contraction of *endogenous morphine.*

enzyme, Chemicals produced by the body to facilitate metabolic chemical reactions. Alcohol dehydrogenase and aldehyde dehydrogenase are the two most involved in alcohol metabolism and related processes.

ester, A class of chemicals formed by the reaction of an acid and an alcohol. Known for their fruity and floral smells, esters occur naturally in many fruits and can be produced from yeast-derived chemicals during fermentation or aging. Particularly associated with rums, wines, and certain beers.

ethanol, The most important ingredient in alcoholic beverages and the primary subject of this book. It is a caloric food, an effective solvent for flavor chemicals, and an irritant to sensitive tissues. Its effects on the central nervous system range from pleasant and relaxing to life threatening, depending on the dose.

fermentation, A category of chemical transformations involving yeasts and bacteria, generally in the context of food and beverages meant for human consumption. Alcoholic drinks, vinegar, sauerkraut, yogurt, and sourdough bread are all produced by fermentation.

formaldehyde, The aldehyde produced by oxidizing or metabolizing methanol. Corrosive, toxic, carcinogenic, and popular as an embalming fluid.

formic acid, The acid produced when formaldehyde is metabolized by aldehyde dehydrogenase. Capable of causing acidification of the blood, oxygen deprivation to the cells, blindness, and lesions on the brain.

fructose, A sugar found in many plants and primarily associated with fruits. Consumption of pure fructose has been shown to speed up ethanol metabolism. It is an isomer of glucose.

fusel alcohol, A class of heavy and often flavorful alcohols produced during fermentation. Concentrated in the tails of a distillation run; may be deliberately incorporated, especially in whiskeys and rums, or discarded.

glucose, A sugar found in many plants and particularly associated with grapes, it is also the main product of carbohydrate digestion. It is an isomer of fructose.

grain alcohol, High-proof neutral spirits derived from cereal grains. Generally about 95 percent alcohol by volume, which is as close to pure ethanol as stills are able to produce in practice.

hemicellulose, A class of organic chemicals that fill in the structural framework of wood and green plants. Consists of chains of sugars (shorter than those in cellulose) so tightly packed as to be indigestible; some sugars are released by burning, producing flavors like those of caramel, which are absorbed into spirits aging in charred or toasted barrels.

hippocampus, A region of the brain involved in forming and storing long-term memories. Its activities are strongly tied to the sense of smell due to its direct connection to the olfactory bulb. Alcohol can interfere with its functioning, particularly if consumed rapidly or in large quantities; in extreme cases, this results in a blackout.

hops, Flowers of the plant *Humulus lupulus*, used as a bittering and flavoring agent in beer. Historically also used for its preservative properties, most famously in India pale ale.

isoamyl acetate, A flavor chemical with a distinct banana aroma. Particularly associated with rum and certain types of beer. Also known as *isopentyl acetate*.

isomer, A compound with the same chemical formula as another compound but a different structure. A common variety is *cis-trans isomerism*, in which the relevant components of the molecule may be either on the same side (the *cis* isomer) or on opposite sides (the *trans* isomer).

lactic acid, A mild acid produced in the course of bacterial fermentation by *Lactobacilli*. It is a distinctive flavor of yogurt, sour cream, sourdough bread, and some beers.

lactone, A class of esters, some of which are aromatic, particularly associated with whiskey. The *oak* or *whiskey lactones*, which are absorbed into aging wines and spirits from the walls of their barrels, have flavors of wood, spice, coconut, and caramel.

lactose, A type of fermentable sugar, found primarily in milk and other dairy products.

lignin, A class of polyphenols that fill in the structural framework of plants, and give strength and hardness to wood. Produces desirable flavor chemicals when burned, including vanillin and clove-like eugenol, which are absorbed into spirits aging in charred or toasted barrels.

limonene, A citrusy terpene present in a variety of fruits and some spices. One of the distinctive flavors of gin.

malic acid, A tart acid found in wines and fruits, especially apples. Winemakers will often induce a secondary *malolactic fermentation* to turn malic acid into lactic acid, which is not as sour.

malt, To cause a cereal grain to sprout, producing enzymes that break the starches down into sugars. A precursor process to the fermentation of grains. Cereal grains prepared in the above manner are called *malts*.

mash, To steep cereal grains in water in preparation for fermentation. Enzymes produced (see *malt*) spread throughout the mixture, converting starches into fermentable sugars. The mixture of water, grains, and (eventually) sugars is known as a *mash*.

Mellanby effect, Reduced impairment at a given blood alcohol level while one is in the process of sobering up, as compared with impairment at the same blood alcohol level reached earlier, while one was in the process of getting drunk.

metabolism, The transformation of chemicals into other chemicals to sustain the life of an organism. May serve the purpose of generating or storing energy, maintaining tissue, removing toxins from the system, etc. A chemical so transformed is said to have been *metabolized*; the by-products of its metabolism are its *metabolites*. The individual processes involved are described as *metabolic*.

methanol, A poisonous alcohol, lethal if consumed in quantity. Metabolized to formaldehyde by alcohol dehydrogenase.

mouthfeel, The tactile elements of a drink, ranging from its viscosity and astringency to the presence of dissolved carbon dioxide and suspended particles. Applies to all beverages, but most frequently used in reference to wines, cocktails, and aged spirits.

muddle, To smash, crush, or grind up sugar, fruit, or leaves in the course of making a cocktail. Done to release essential oils or make the ingredients easier to incorporate into the liquid. The tool used, called a *muddler*, resembles a large pestle.

nucleation sites, The discrete points at which a substance collects in the course of being removed from a solution or undergoing a change in thermodynamic phase. Examples include bubbles of carbon dioxide in beer, bubbles of vapor in boiling water, and the imperfections in the glass or pot from which individual streams of bubbles rise. The overall phenomenon, called *nucleation*, is also responsible for the formation of clouds

oenology, The scientific study of wine and winemaking. A person engaged in this field is an *oenologist*. Also spelled *enology* and *enologist*.

olfaction, The technical term for the sense of smell. Smelling chemicals through the nose is *orthonasal olfaction*, while smelling those that waft up from the back of the throat into the nasal cavity is *retronasal olfaction*.

olfactory bulb, The primary organ involved in the sense of smell. A part of the forebrain, it has direct connections to the olfactory sensors in the nasal cavity and the seats of visceral memory in the hippocampus and amygdala.

organic molecule, A molecule containing carbon, particularly one produced by a living organism. Definitions vary but may require the carbon atom(s) to be bonded to hydrogen atoms or to other carbon atoms in a chain. Alcohols, aldehydes, enzymes, proteins, fats, and carbohydrates are examples of organic molecules.

orthonasal olfaction, see *olfaction*

overproof, Having a proof greater than 100°. Most often applies to whiskeys and rums.

oxidize, To change a molecule chemically by adding an oxygen atom, removing a hydrogen atom, or causing it to lose electrons, depending on the context. The process is called *oxidation*; many of the flavor changes in aged spirits take place by means of oxidation, as does the body's metabolism of ethanol.

phenol, A class of chemicals containing a hydroxyl group (an oxygen molecule connected to a hydrogen molecule) bonded to an aromatic hydrocarbon group (a ring of carbon atoms bonded to hydrogen atoms and each other). Molecules that contain many iterations of this structure may be called *polyphenols*.

placebo, A substance not known to have medical effects that is administered under the pretext that it does. If the patient experiences the stated effects, the cause is believed to be psychological; this phenomenon is called the *placebo effect*.

polyphenol, *see phenol*

proof, A unit of strength for alcoholic beverages, particularly distilled spirits. The proof measurement is equal to twice the alcohol percentage by volume; a whiskey that is 50 percent alcohol by volume would be 100 proof. Often indicated with the degree symbol (°).

pyloric sphincter, The muscle that opens or closes the passage from the stomach to the small intestine.

reflux, The cycle of evaporation and condensation that takes place in a still. Some stills are designed to maximize reflux.

retrograde amnesia, see *anterograde amnesia*

retronasal olfaction, see *olfaction*

saccharification, The process by which a complex carbohydrate (a *starch*) is broken down into simple carbohydrates (*sugars*). A necessary step in fermenting starchy grains, usually accomplished by malting or the introduction of other microorganisms.

solvent, A substance that dissolves something else. Ordinarily the solvent is a liquid, and the substance dissolved in it (the *solute*) is a solid or a gas. Water and ethanol are solvents.

tannin, A type of polyphenol strongly associated with red wine but also found in barrel-aged spirits. Contributes astringency and bitterness; a beverage with these characteristics may be described as *tannic*.

terpene, A class of strong-smelling chemicals that may smell flowery, woody, citrusy, or minty. Particularly prominent in the flavor profiles of gins.

trans isomer, see *isomer*

vanillin, The distinctive flavor of vanilla; also produced by toasting wood and therefore found in barrel-aged wines and spirits.

vasodilation, The widening of blood vessels, resulting in increased blood flow and lower blood pressure in the affected area. Commonly triggered by exercise, heat, and the ingestion of ethanol or chili peppers.

volatile, Of a molecule, having a strong tendency to escape from the surface of a liquid as vapor. Aromatic chemicals tend to possess this characteristic (otherwise they couldn't be smelled); those in a particular beverage are often referred to as the *volatile aromatics* or simply the *volatiles* by a brewer, distiller, or bartender.

Notes

1: Fermentation

1. The physics of the sticky wave of death itself, while fascinating, are beyond the scope of this book. Interested readers should consult Jabr, "The Science of the Great Molasses Flood."

2. For more on this experiment, and on the mysteries of terroir, check out McGee and Patterson, "Talk Dirt to Me."

2: Distillation

1. These idiosyncracies have consequences. In 1996, Heaven Hill Distilleries had a fire and had to move their production to another site with different stills; even though they kept making their whiskey the same way, it came out tasting different. Adam Rogers tells this story much better than I can, in *Proof*, p. 94–100.

3: Aging

1. For this discussion of oak-wood and its chemicals and flavor properties, I've leaned heavily on McGee, *On Food and Cooking*, p. 720–22, and on U.S. Forestry Service, "Oak Aging and Wine."

2. No, really. See U.S. Code of Federal Regulations, Title 27: Alcohol, Tobacco Products and Firearms, Part 5—Labeling and Advertising of Distilled Spirits, Subpart C—Standards of Identity for Distilled Spirits. If you're really into spirits or really into law, the U.S. Code makes for fascinating reading.

3. *Baudoinia* is neat. It grows even on glass and stainless steel. Its whole branch of the fungal family tree likes extreme conditions; one cousin lives in Antarctica. For more, see Rogers, *Proof*, p. 104–8, 115–19; and

Scott et al., "*Baudoinia*: A New Genus to Accommodate *Torula compniacensis*."

4. *Palette* isn't a typo—I'm thinking of a painter's palette of colors, rather than the taste (*palate*) of a drink, since we're talking about a variety of ingredients without flavors of their own.

5. It's probably worth noting that most of the plants we eat in practice have another reason to be tasty: thousands of years of selective breeding by human farmers. It's a great evolutionary strategy for the affected plants—without people there would be no apples in Ohio and no tomatoes in Italy.

6. If the reader is interested in infusing at home, I highly recommend checking out the recipes developed by the grain alcohol manufacturer Everclear. The company has hired no less talented a mixologist than Ted Kilgore (co-owner of Planter's House in St. Louis and a formidable cocktail writer in his own right) to come up with recipes for homemade liqueurs using grain alcohol; they are invariably excellent and quite inexpensive to produce.

4: Preparation

1. One other fun fact about beer bubbles, and bubbles in general: we think of them as inevitably rising, because they're lighter than the liquid that contains them, but they can sink, too.

Bubbles on the sides of a vessel tend to move more slowly than ones in the middle, because they keep getting attracted to the glass. As the ones in the middle move up, they displace liquid, which has to go somewhere. The path of least resistance sometimes means moving out to the sides, where the slower-moving bubbles generate less pressure, and the additional weight of liquid causes them to sink.

2. There isn't a lot of literature on the phenomenon of the freeing of volatiles by a splash of water, but the aroma-suppressing effects of wood lignin in ethanol have been documented. Whether that's a good thing or a bad thing probably depends on the particular spirit and your tastes; see Conner et al., "Release of Distillate Flavour Compounds in Scotch Malt Whisky." As for ethanol and water generating heat when mixed together, it's weird to me, too, but apparently the case; see Peeters and Huyskens, "Endothermicity or Exothermicity of Water/Alcohol Mixtures," and "Bowmore and Water" on the Bowmore website.

3. See Jack, "Development of Guidelines for the Preparation and Handling of Sensory Samples in the Scotch Whisky Industry."

4. See Cui et al., "Simultaneous Determination of 20 Components in Red Wine by LC-MS."

5. To put a finer point on it, the Centers for Disease Control estimates that 1.2 million people in the United States will be infected with *Salmonella* in a given year. That sounds like a lot, until you realize that only 450 of those will be fatal cases (most likely in children, the elderly, and the immunocompromised); that many of those cases have nothing to do with eggs; and that the Department of Transportation's National Highway Traffic Safety Administration reported over two million injuries and more than thirty thousand deaths in car accidents for 2013.

6. Dave Arnold has done a scary amount of research on ice science and is my primary source for this section; see *Liquid Intelligence*, especially p. 74, 80, and 87–88; and "Tales of the Cocktail: Science of Shaking II."

7. Arnold is quick to point out, in "Science of Shaking II," that your ice and shaking style are sure to affect the drink and its presentation in other ways.

8. Arnold suggests straining crushed ice; he stops short of advocating a run through a salad spinner, even though he obviously wants to. Since I assume most readers of this book will find either technique to be more hassle than they're looking for, I recommend avoiding crushed ice except in the rare drink that specifically calls for it, like the highly boozy Mint Julep.

9. Incidentally, many more herbs than you might think are members of either the mint family (e.g., oregano and basil) or the carrot family (parsley and dill).

10. Kevin Liu is one of these advocates; see *Craft Cocktails at Home*, p. 73.

11. OK, the mint leaf is the Mint Julep's most important *orthonasal* olfactory element. *Retronasal* olfaction proceeds as normal. Have a look at "Taste, Smell, and the Evolution of a Sip" in Chapter 5 (p. 95) if you have no idea what those words mean.

5: Sip

1. You may have heard the word *umami*, which is very hip right now. It's a Japanese term used to describe a savory taste; for the purposes of this book, I'm cutting out the middleman and sticking with "savory."

2. For a somewhat related discussion, take a look at this scientific investigation of various mouthfeel characteristics in thirty different beers, Langstaff and Lewis, "The Mouthfeel of Beer."

3. See, for instance, Gibbins and Carpenter, "Alternative Mechanisms of Astringency."

It's worth noting that there has been *substantial* scientific head scratching on the topic of astringency. The literature is a bit muddled, and some very intelligent minds are skeptical of the protein-stripping explanation. I use it because it makes intuitive sense and still appears to fit the phenomenon better than the alternatives, but if you're curious, I encourage you to make use of one of these surveys to get a full sense of the debate. Some people even think astringency is a sixth taste (at least in rats): see Bajec and Pickering, "Astringency: Mechanisms and Perception"; and Chen and Engelen, *Food Oral Processing*, p. 284.

4. See Wise et al., "The Influence of Bubbles on the Perception Carbonation Bite."

5. See Morrot et al., "The Color of Odors."

6. I'm speaking from personal experience here, but if you'd like confirmation that this isn't unique to me and my friends, or particular to one brand of crème de violette, see "Crème de Violette," *Hunger and Thirst*. The author of this blog makes a homemade version and describes its flavor the same way.

7. Experiments have been done to confirm that these brain regions are not only connected to the olfactory bulb but activated when memories are triggered by smell; see Herz et al., "Neuroimaging Evidence for the Emotional Potency of Odor-Evoked Memory."

8. What is probably the best-known example of the scent-emotion connection is a fictional one, the scene in Marcel Proust's

In Search of Lost Time that made the madeleine famous as a memory trigger.

9. For the Caltech/Stanford study, see Plassmann et al., "Marketing Actions Can Modulate Neural Representations of Experienced Pleasantness."

10. The difference between the reactions of wine experts and nonexperts is really quite substantial. Generalizing to a 100-point rating scale, and considering two wines—one of which is ten times costlier than the other—the average person will rate the more expensive wine four points lower than the cheaper one, while the professionals will rate it seven points higher; see Goldstein et al., "Do More Expensive Wines Taste Better?"

These results have since been reinforced by another experiment, which found a neutral to negative effect of increasing price on wine enjoyment; see Ashton, "Wine as an Experience Good."

11. For the Yale study, see Cruz and Green, "Thermal Stimulation of Taste"; for a summary, see Peart, "Study Shows Tongue's Temperature Affects Taste."

6: Metabolism of Alcohol

1. See Roine et al., "Effect of Concentration of Ingested Ethanol on Blood Alcohol Levels."

2. For the Swedish study, see Jones and Jönsson, "Food-

induced Lowering of Blood-Ethanol Profiles and Increased Rate of Elimination Immediately after a Meal."

3. See Jones et al., "Effect of High-Fat, High-Protein, and High-Carbohydrate Meals on the Pharmacokinetics of a Small Dose of Ethanol."

4. See Hunt and Knox, "A Relation between the Chain Length of Fatty Acids and the Slowing of Gastric Emptying."

5. See Meyer et al., "The Effect of Fructose on Blood Alcohol Levels in Man."

6. A very heavily simplified explanation for how fructose affects BAC: Ethanol metabolism involves nicotinamide adenine dinucleotide (NAD), moving from its oxidized form, NAD+, to its reduced form, NADH. That, in turn, means you can metabolize ethanol in proportion only with the NAD+ you have available. Fructose helps turn some of that NADH back into NAD+; it's like a hybrid car turning a waste product into something it can use. See Parlesaka et al., "First-Pass Metabolism of Ethanol in Human Beings: Effect of Intravenous Infusion of Fructose." For a confirming study see Mascord et al., "The Effect of Fructose on Alcohol Metabolism and on the [Lactate]/[Pyruvate] Ratio in Man."

7. See Petersen et al., "Effect of Local Controlled Heat on Transdermal Delivery of Nicotine."

8. For the hot-meal study, see Bateman, "Effects of Meal Temperature and Volume on the Emptying of Liquid from the Human Stomach."

9. See Bailey et al., "Ethanol Enhances the Hemodynamic Effects of Felodipine."

10. Most of the work of ethanol metabolism is done by alcohol dehydrogenase. Cytochrome P450 2E1 is the only relative of CYP3A4 known to be involved in ethanol metabolism, but it comes into play primarily at high alcohol concentrations and doesn't have any known interactions with grapefruit juice.

11. For the vodka and tonic study see Whitehouse, "'Fake Alcohol' Can Make You Tipsy."

12. See Lang et al., "Effects of Alcohol on Aggression in Male Social Drinkers"; and George and Marlatt, "The Effects of Alcohol and Anger on Interest in Violence, Erotica, and Deviance."

13. See Attwood et al., "Glass Shape Influences Consumption Rate for Alcoholic Beverages."

14. See Guéguen et al., "Sound Level of Environmental Music and Drinking Behavior."

15. For the Italian study, see Frezza et al., "High Blood Alcohol Levels in Women." For a confirming study, see Baraona et al.,

"Gender Differences in Pharmacokinetics of Alcohol."

16. See Wynne et al., "The Association of Age with the Activity of Alcohol Dehydrogenase in Human Liver"; Chumlea et al., "Total Body Water Data for White Adults 18 to 64 Years of Age"; and Seitz et al., "Human Gastric Alcohol Dehydrogenase Activity: Effect of Age, Sex, and Alcoholism."

17. See Wroblewski et al., "Chronic Exercise Preserves Lean Muscle Mass in Masters Athletes."

7: Effects

1. Many people, myself included, drink for many other reasons, flavor chief among them. But we obviously enjoy the buzz, too.

2. The statement "alcohol makes you feel good" assumes that your body produces alcohol dehydrogenase and aldehyde dehydrogenase in the right ratio. See "Ethanol Metabolism," in the Appendix.

3. See Mitchell et al., "Alcohol Consumption Induces Endogenous Opioid Release in the Human Orbitofrontal Cortex and Nucleus Accumbens"; or, for a summary, see O'Brien, "Study Offers Clue As to Why Alcohol Is Addicting."

4. The neurobiology is of course far more complicated than this, and beyond the scope of this

book. See Galanter, *The American Psychiatric Publishing Textbook of Substance Abuse Treatment.*

5. Even this is a simplification. The inner ear is really complicated.

6. This is called the "buoyancy hypothesis"; see Brandt, "Positional Nystagmus/Vertigo with Specific Gravity Differential Between Cupula and Endolymph (Buoyancy Hypothesis)."

7. It's probably worth noting that Dean Martin wasn't actually the alcoholic he appeared to be in public; he was as likely to be drinking apple juice as hard liquor while he was working. Heavy drinking was simply part of his persona, as it was for Winston Churchill, Ernest Hemingway, and many other people who have led notoriously wet lives.

8. For the study on mice, see Ozburn et al., "Chronic Voluntary Alcohol Consumption Results in Tolerance to Sedative/Hypnotic and Hypothermic Effects of Alcohol in Hybrid Mice."

9. See Mellanby, "Alcohol: Its Absorption into and Disappearance from Blood Under Different Conditions"; cited in Moskowitz et al., "The Mellanby Effect in Moderate and Heavy Drinkers."

10. Depending on the sobriety test administered, it's conceivable that the improved performance could be the result of the subject having learned to per-

form the tasks better, but studies that control for such a possibility have turned up equally clear results; see Moskowitz et al., "The Mellanby Effect."

11. For the study, see Beirness and Vogel-Sprott, "Alcohol Tolerance in Social Drinkers." There is significant corroborating evidence that some element of tolerance both for ethanol and for a variety of other drugs is a result of learning and adaptation. It's well beyond the scope of this book, but there's a good overview in Goudie and Emmett-Oglesby, "Alcohol."

12. Caffeine and heroin also cross the blood-brain barrier without much trouble; doing so is a useful ability for a drug that wants to be popular. See Banks, "Characteristics of Compounds that Cross the Blood-Brain Barrier"; and Frankenheim and Brown, *Bioavailability of Drugs to the Brain and the Blood–Brain Barrier.*

13. For more on BAC and BrAC, take a spin through the National Safety Council's fascinating and extensive *History of the Committee on Alcohol and Other Drugs.*

14. For the British study see Alobaidi et al., "Significance of Variations in Blood: Breath Partition Coefficient of Alcohol"; for the Croatian study see Vukovic et al., "Comparison of Breath and Blood Alcohol Concentrations in a Controlled Drinking Study."

15. According to Siegel and Mirakovits, *Forensic Science: The Basics,* the U.S. state of Oklahoma has a BrAC-based statute and instruments that don't even bother converting BrAC to BAC. It's the same imperfect metric everybody else is actually using, but at least Oklahoma's lawmakers are being upfront about it.

16. This caloric supplementation was then repeated with two thousand calories of chocolate, with more predictable results. Brody, "Why the Body May Waste the Calories from Alcohol," in the *New York Times,* gives a good summary; for the original study see Lieber, "Perspectives: Do Alcohol Calories Count?"

17. See Gillespie, "Vasodilator Properties of Alcohol."

18. See Suddendorf, "Research on Alcohol Metabolism among Asians and Its Implications for Understanding Causes of Alcoholism."
It has been suggested that acetaldehyde is predominantly responsible for the milder variants of these symptoms that we all experience while drinking, and that ethanol either is not involved or plays only a minor role. This passes the smell test and fits the principle of Occam's razor, but it's also very difficult to study.

19. See Holdstock and de Wit, "Individual Differences in the Biphasic Effects of Ethanol."

20. Anticipation effects in rats have been studied a lot. See Melendez et al., "Microdialysis of Dopamine in the Nucleus Accumbens of Alcohol-Preferring (P) Rats during Anticipation and Operant Self-Administration of Ethanol"; and Weiss et al., "Oral Alcohol Self-Administration Stimulates Dopamine Release in the Rat Nucleus Accumbens."

21. It will probably not surprise you to learn that this is a dramatic oversimplification and that research into and debate about ethanol's effects on GABA activity are ongoing. See, for example, Valenzuela, "Alcohol and Neurotransmitter Interactions"; Davies, "The role of GABA$_A$ Receptors in Mediating the Effects of Alcohol in the Central Nervous System"; and National Institute on Alcohol and Alcoholism, "Neuroscience Research and Therapeutic Targets."

On the other hand, it may surprise you to learn that the bodies of long-term heavy drinkers attempt to compensate for the increased inhibitory response, essentially adapting to the constant presence of alcohol. If they go cold turkey, the net result is too much excitability in the nervous system, which is, at least in broad strokes, why alcoholics get the shakes and why seizures can be a symptom of severe alcohol withdrawal. See Trevisan et al., "Complications of Alcohol Withdrawal"; and Brailowsky and García, "Ethanol, GABA and Epilepsy."

22. This information on the efficacy of a nightcap as a sleep aid comes from a literature review by those notorious drink pushers at the National Institute on Alcohol Abuse and Alcoholism (NIAAA). Seriously, though, their website is probably the best one-stop shop out there for information on alcohol's effects, whether good or bad; see Roehrs and Roth, "Sleep, Sleepiness, and Alcohol Use."

23. Drinking also messes with the balance of REM (rapid-eye-movement, or dreaming) sleep, and SWS (slow-wave, or deep) sleep, but the manner and significance aren't fully understood, even by people much smarter than you and me.

24. It's worth noting that there is reason to be skeptical of such a success rate in the long term, because people have a tendency to develop a tolerance to ethanol, and, to state the obvious, booze has other effects on you besides putting you to sleep. Unfortunately we don't have much academic literature on the many, many peripheral questions raised by using ethanol to treat insomnia. I have interpolated diagnostic criteria for insomnia from the *Diagnostic and Statistical Manual of Mental Disorders*, 5th ed. (DSM-5); see American Psychiatric Association, "Sleep-Wake Disorders Fact Sheet." The

DSM-4 criteria for "primary insomnia," the term used in the NIAAA literature review (see note 22), can be found in Harvard Medical School Department of Health Care Policy, "DSM-IV-TR Diagnostic Criteria for Primary Insomnia."

25. For the rehab study, see O'Keefe and D. K., "Assessment and Treatment of Impotence," which was quoted in Wagner and Saenz de Tejada, "Update on Male Erectile Dysfunction." For the chronic users' problems, see Arackal and Benegal, "Prevalence of Sexual Dysfunction in Male Subjects with Alcohol Dependence."

26. For the study of moderate drinkers see George et al., "Alcohol and Erectile Response: The Effects of High Dosage in the Context of Demands to Maximize Sexual Arousal."

27. My explanation of the myopia theory is drastically simplified, of course, but it'll do for our purposes. For more, see the original paper: Steele and Josephs, "Alcohol Myopia. Its Prized and Dangerous Effects"; as well as Giancola et al., "Alcohol Myopia Revisited: Clarifying Aggression and Other Acts of Disinhibition through a Distorted Lens," a 2010 update taking subsequent studies into account. For more on alcohol myopia and risky sexual behavior specifically, see MacDonald et al., "Alcohol, Sexual Arousal, and Intentions to

Use Condoms in Young Men: Applying Alcohol Myopia Theory to Risky Sexual Behavior."

28. See Chivers et al., "Agreement of Self-Reported and Genital Measures of Sexual Arousal in Men and Women."

29. I'm leaning heavily on the NIAAA's survey of blackout literature for this section. If you'd like more information on any topic, unless I've specified otherwise I recommend reading that document and probing its source material; White, "What Happened? Alcohol, Memory Blackouts, and the Brain."

30. For the study, see Goodwin et al., "Loss of Short Term Memory as a Predictor of the Alcoholic 'Blackout'" (quoted in the NIAAA review).

31. For the study of hospitalized alcoholics, see Goodwin et al., "Alcoholic 'Blackouts': A Review and Clinical Study of 100 Alcoholics"; for the study of college students, see White et al., "Prevalence and Correlates of Alcohol-Induced Blackouts among College Students."

32. For a discussion of this study and several others, see Calder, "Hangovers: Not the Ethanol— Perhaps the Methanol."

33. See Maxwell et al., "Acetate Causes Alcohol Hangover Headache in Rats."

34. For the report on people given tolfenamic acid, see Kai-

vola, et al., "Hangover Headache and Prostaglandins: Prophylactic Treatment with Tolfenamic Acid." Tolfenamic acid is the strongest candidate I've found for a hangover cure—or a hangover vaccine, I suppose, because we know for sure only that it works if taken prophylactically. Unfortunately, if you'd like to try it yourself, you'll have to hop across the pond: it's readily available in the United Kingdom as a migraine medicine but not so easy to come by in the United States.

A Nightcap

1. See Hockings, et al., "Tools to Tipple: Ethanol Ingestion by Wild Chimpanzees Using Leaf-Sponges"; and Gill, "Chimpanzees Found to Drink Alcoholic Plant Sap in Wild."

2. The BBC has spectacular footage of this online; see, for example, "Alcoholic Vervet Monkeys! – Weird Nature – BBC Animals," on YouTube.

3. Along with Rainier, the authorities used doughnuts and honey—or as we call it at my house, "the breakfast of champions."

4. Sadly, much of our evidence for bird drunkenness comes from finding dead birds. They can get so drunk they fly into things or fall out of trees; if you see a fruit-eating bird inexplicably lying on the ground, it might be a casualty of an alcohol-induced avian accident. In less sad news, it's believed that waxwings have larger livers to accommodate their wet winter lifestyle.

5. If you're like me, reading about the studies that people have gotten to conduct on the effects of alcohol has stirred your sense of envy. The zebra finch experiment is one that I wish I could have conducted, and it's also unquestionably the most adorable study in the entire book. To read the study, see Olson et al., "Drinking Songs: Alcohol Effects on Learned Song of Zebra Finches"; to hear side-by-side comparisons of the sober and drunken finch song on NPR, in an interview with the study team's leader, follow the link at Hopkins, "Scientists Discover That Drunk Birds Sing Like Drunks."

Bibliography

General references for the book are listed here. For a full list of references by chapter, please visit http://www.herzogcocktailschool.com/distilled-knowledge.

Arnold, Dave. *Liquid Intelligence: The Art and Science of the Perfect Cocktail*. New York: W. W. Norton, 2014.

Barth, Roger. *The Chemistry of Beer: The Science in the Suds*. Hoboken, NJ: John Wiley and Sons, 2013.

Embury, David. *The Fine Art of Mixing Drinks*. New York: Mud Puddle Books, 2009.

Goode, Jamie. *The Science of Wine*. Berkeley and Los Angeles: University of California Press, 2005.

Halliday, James, and Hugh Johnson. *The Art and Science of Wine*. Buffalo, NY: Firefly Books, 2007.

Liu, Kevin. *Craft Cocktails at Home*. Published by the author, 2013.

McGee, Harold. *On Food and Cooking: The Science and Lore of the Kitchen*. New York: Scribner, 2004.

Rogers, Adam. *Proof: The Science of Booze*. New York: Houghton Mifflin Harcourt, 2014.

Spoelman, Colin, and David Haskell. *The Kings County Distillery Guide to Urban Moonshining: How to Make and Drink Whiskey*. New York: Abrams, 2013.

Watson, Ronald Ross, Victor R. Preedy, and Sherma Zibadi. *Alcohol, Nutrition, and Health Consequences*. New York: Humana Press, 2013.

Wondrich, David. *Imbibe! From Absinthe Cocktail to Whiskey Smash, a Salute in Stories and Drinks to "Professor" Jerry Thomas, Pioneer of the American Bar*. New York: Penguin Group, 2015.

Index

Acknowledgments

I could never seriously claim that this book was the product of my labor and no one else's. The dedicated scientists, writers, and liquor-industry professionals who study the topics covered in this book paved the way for *Distilled Knowledge* without knowing it, and I'm grateful to them collectively for their work to expand the boundaries of human knowledge.

There are, however, some people who merit individual recognition, to whom I would now like to extend my thanks:

First and foremost, to Robert Abrams, the founder of Abbeville Press, for taking a chance on this book and on me.

To those people who have encouraged me in my cocktail business and other quixotic pursuits; in particular Allie Anderson, Tim Cabral, Josh Childs, Chris Ell, Jon Rubin, Clare Sachsse, Ryan Stephan, Michael Ambrose Stevens, and Barbara Tellalian.

To Barbara Ligon, who told me many years ago, point-blank, that I needed to learn how to write, and took up the challenge of teaching me.

To Tristyn Bloom and Max Jacobson, who have always had more confidence in my writing than I have; and to George Donnelly and Matthew Schmitz for getting me started in this line of work.

To Jackson Cannon, Kirie Stromberg, Graham Wright, and Fred Yarm, without whom the happy accidents that produced this book would never have come to pass.

To those widely varied institutions that have afforded me the best writing environments, in particular 11 Story Street, Amtrak, the Boston Athenaeum, and Silvertone Bar and Grill.

To John Harvey, for his invaluable technical assistance.

To Misha Beletsky, who designed the book, and Louise Kurtz, who coordinated its production. They are the unsung heroes of this process, without whom *Distilled Knowledge* would be a loose pile of unadorned papers. And to the rest of the ever-wonderful Abbeville team, in particular Nicole Lanctot, Carolina Ortiz, and Nadine Winns.

To all those who have assisted me in researching and writing this book, in particular Andrew McCabe, Ian McLaren, Steve Neidhardt, Paul Norris, Catherine Piccoli, Kerri Platt, Paul Rothenberg, Amy Stewart, Alejandro Torres, Rita Watson, and Richard Zare; as well as Astraluna, Dirty Water Distillery, Kings County Distillery, GrandTen Distilling, the Museum of Food and Drink, Elsevier, Bacardi, and Patrón Tequila.

To my copy editor, Amy Hughes, and my thoughtful and extremely necessary fact-checkers, Elizabeth Aslinger, James Cucchi, Kyle Killeen, Regina Lief, and Keith Parker, without whose assistance God only knows what might have made it in here.

To my family, for their unwavering support.

To my extraordinarily tolerant roommate, Caroline Fenn, for allowing me to bounce ideas off of her at whatever odd times they happened to come to me, and for putting up with me with more grace than she should ever have had occasion to show.

To Leandro Castelao, the humble, hard-working genius who has turned my needlessly wordy descriptions and chicken-scratch sketches into the gorgeous illustrations in these pages. This is his book as much as it is mine.

Most of all, to Shannon Lee Connors, my editor, life coach, and very dear friend. It's true that this book wouldn't be what it is without her steady hand and editorial guidance, but that's hardly sufficient praise. Without Shannon, there would be no book. Her faith and determination did more to turn an idle thought into a printed volume than I ever did. The idea was mine, but the vision was hers. However much credit she's given for this book, it will never be enough.

About the Author

Brian D. Hoefling is a cocktail historian, instructor, and inveterate barfly. The founder of the Herzog Cocktail School and a specialist in custom cocktail courses, his writing has appeared in the *Boston Business Journal*. He lives in Cambridge, Massachusetts with an impressive selection of rums. For more information, visit him at herzogcocktailschool.com/distilledknowledge.

About the Illustrator

Leandro Castelao is an Argentinian illustrator based in Brooklyn, New York. He has worked with the *New York Times*, the *New Yorker*, Nike, and Google, among many others. In 2014 he was nominated for a Latin Grammy Award for best recording packaging. Visit him at leandrocastelao.com.

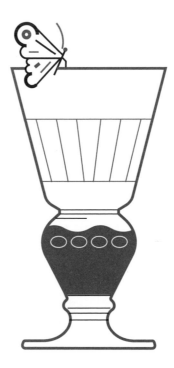